The 24-Hour Christian

Sheer Encouragement for the Christian in the World

Earl F. Palmer

Regent College Publishing
Vancouver

First published 1987 by InterVarsity Press, P.O. Box 1400, Downers
Grove, IL 60515 U.S.A.

This edition published 2001 by Regent College Publishing
5800 University Boulevard, Vancouver, B.C. Canada V6T 2E4
www.regentpublishing.com

The views expressed in works published by Regent College Publishing
are those of the author and do not necessarily represent the official
position of Regent College.

The paper used in this publication meets the minimum requirements of
the American National Standard for Information Sciences —
Permanence of Paper for Printed Library Materials, ANSI Z39.48-1984.

National Library of Canada Cataloguing in Publication Data

Palmer, Earl F.
  The 24-hour Christian

  ISBN 1-55361-037-7 (Canada)
  ISBN 1-57383-222-7 (United States)

  1. Christian life. I. Title. II. Title: Twenty-four hour Christian.
BV4501.2.P34 2001   248.8'4   C2001-911499-0

For Elizabeth,
daughter and friend

Preface

This is a book both for those who are Christians and for those who are not now or not yet Christians. It is, I hope, a realistic look at the claims and promises of the Christian faith from the viewpoint of the living place—the place each of us lives our lives—the 24-hour cycle we share with every other human being.

This book is about mentoring, and, though students and young adult readers may find these chapters especially relevant, the themes and the point of view are transgenerational. I have learned from my own life story that mentoring happens in both directions between the generations. Students have mentored me as much as I have mentored them, especially the three in my own family: Anne, in her second year in medical school; Jon, a university senior in international relations; and Elizabeth, a junior in high school.

These young adults, with their own journeys of faith and their common thread of honesty and love for people and their eagerness for adventures, have wonderfully encouraged and mentored their parents Shirley and me. Within the 24-hour cycle of our lives, we all owe a debt to each other for the gift of encouragement.

Sheer encouragement, that special affirmation that is found in mentors, is really what this book is about. In my own journey I have had mentors at each of the key transitional turning places, and most of these people have never been aware of the important role that they have played in my life: Dallas U. Birch who made me feel good about myself as a young boy; my mother and father who always encouraged me to think for myself; Mrs. Gerlicher who in high school convinced me that I was smart; Arba Hudgens in college who first invited me into Christian fellowship; Rev. Bob Munger who as my pastor modeled integrity in ministry; John A. Mackay who showed to me the vast dimensions of the kingly reign of Christ; Henrietta Mears who made me feel special; Dick Jacobson who was a true friend; Dale Bruner who encouraged me to teach; Floyd Thatcher who encouraged me to write; Bill Miller for loyalty, Peter Yuen for sheer honesty, David Gill for healthy boldness and John Blaul for courage. My life is richer for these men and women who I found and who found me. Perhaps you as a reader will write your own list before too many pages.

Earl Palmer
Berkeley, California
May 1987

Introduction: The Christian Mentor

Discoveries—we make them all of our lives. But some of the most important occur when we are very young. They may be good or they may be harmful, but when we are young every discovery— good and bad—bears one mark: tremendous authority.

As children we are instinctively oriented toward the authority of parents, teachers and friends. We trust quickly and deeply. We assume that those discoveries we make when we are young will stay unchanged and permanently in place. Such is the nature of the beginning stages of our intellectual and convictional life.

Nothing Stays Put

But we soon discover that our convictions are not as durable as we thought. As Pascal said, "Nothing stays put for us." One of the most important surprises of adolescence and young adulthood is the shaking and upsetting of earlier strong opinions and of conclusions we were once so sure of.

At some point we all identify with the marvelously funny yet sadly wistful soliloquy of the King in *The King and I:* "I wish I was more certain of the things I absolutely know . . . some things nearly so, some things nearly not." What we thought would never change does change, often right in front of our eyes.

Three Phases of the Human Pilgrimage
The teen-age years of the high-schooler and college student become a time for the negotiation of values. Earlier beliefs and points of view are held at bay, weighed and tested. Convictions are newly formed, values framed and a foundation laid on which we continue to build our lives from then on.

But this testing doesn't conclude with adulthood. Each of us journeys along this pathway long after the teen-age years. And the results are as different as the journeyers. Throughout our lives we continue the discovering and the negotiating, the building and the rebuilding.

There are three phases in the human pilgrimage that I have just described. First is *discovery*. What does a person learn in the first place? How substantial is the discovery? How well will its truth stand up to the inevitable testing that lies ahead?

Second are the *convictions* we finally decide to live with. These are the philosophical and personal building stones that we chose to keep as a part of the house we are building once we move through the process of negotiation.

And third is the *negotiation process* itself. How does this negotiation take place? How are values previously discovered actively sorted through and weighed?

Mentors and Teachers
In the time of sorting each of us needs a mentor—someone to

stand alongside as a positive reference point, a special soul mate we can trust.

By mentor, I do not mean one more authority figure like the ones we meet at the beginning of our pilgrimage. They were necessary during the discovery period. Someone had to clue us in at the very beginning. But just as we needed an evangelist who invited us into relationship with God, so even during the negotiation period, we continue to need teachers and others—prophets who warn and cheer us, and priests to encourage by prayer and ongoing care. None of us develops values in a vacuum. More important at this stage, however, is the genuine mentor, a clarifier, an encourager, one who helps us think through our own thoughts.

A mentor's advice is different from a teacher's; it is the counsel that works with the knowledge we already have. The distinctive mark of mentoring advice is that it is integrative. It takes what we know and moves on from there.

J. R. R. Tolkien once described C. S. Lewis, a friend who was also a mentor to him:

> The unpayable debt that I owe to him was not influence as it is ordinarily understood, but sheer encouragement. He for a long time was my only audience. Only from him did I ever get the idea that my 'stuff' could be more than a private hobby.

"Sheer encouragement." Yes, that is the role a mentor plays for us. Lewis does not begin Tolkien's journey nor could he dominate Tolkien or even teach him the things to write about. Rather, he played another role: he encouraged Tolkien to keep on writing when he thought about stopping; he encouraged Tolkien to try out his "stuff" with publishers when Tolkien had lost confidence in himself and his work. Lewis helped Tolkien to sort through and weigh the thoughts he already had found and was finding.

Each of us needs mentors who not so much teach us first principles as encourage us to remember those we have already learned. Mentors do not so much create new ideas as work with ones that have already broken through into our consciousness and are now being negotiated.

Though a mentor may often be a teacher—or evangelist, prophet or priest—to us, the roles are different. When mentoring begins to happen in the relationship of teacher and student, there is a shift of weight. An odd kind of equality and evenness becomes evident, a change in presence. Fathers and mothers, grandfathers and grandmothers may also become mentors as they have the wisdom to shift weight and balance in their relationship with the growing person who is their offspring.

I have mentors and their words and friendships have been and are intellectually and spiritually helpful at very impressionable times in my life. Their advice plays an integrative role for my mind and heart.

The Role of a Mentor

Of course, not all advice is useful, and some of it may be confusing, but this does not mean that a Christian is better off isolated from all counsel. When we are isolated, then it is our own advice—our own thoughts, our own feelings—that we hear too much and too loudly. The advice we give to ourselves is uneven at best. We have no way of really knowing how clearly we have understood what needs to be understood. We have no way to assess when we are too easy or too hard on ourselves. It takes a vantage point different from our own to see the shades of color, the ambiguities that are so essential as the background for the most brilliant colors.

What, for example, we may interpret in ourselves as singular cowardice may really be a shared human weakness—or a wise judgment at a dangerous moment. It often takes a mentor to help us distinguish truly and to supply a necessary reality check.

On the other hand, a mentor can be the reference pointer who helps us to face squarely quite a different possibility. What we might tell ourselves is "a necessary reaction to a dangerous and threatening situation" perhaps more realistically should be described as "an act of cowardice." The mentor in each instance is a friend who offers the sheer encouragement of supportive clarity—for us and not against us, alongside of us and not over against us.

A Mentor Is Chosen
Here is another distinction. Often we do not choose our teachers—or the evangelist who seeks us out, or the prophets and priests who help us, and certainly not our parents. But we always choose our mentors, and this gives them a unique value. In this way a mentor offers a sort of influence in our spiritual pilgrimage different from other influential people and institutions.

Think of this in the context of our Christian lives. The evangelist finds us and proclaims the message of the hope of the gospel. The prophet proclaims the implications of the kingly reign of Jesus Christ toward us and our generation. The pastor/priest ministers to the real needs that he or she perceives in us as they come alongside of our lives and offer their prayers for us and the good help that is the result of the gospel. Teachers teach us the meaning of the gospel; they win our respect by the thoughtful way they make truth accessible to our minds. But we must find on our own someone to help us negotiate all the input we now possess so that we can make it on our own. In short, we must find our own mentors.

A mentor may be an evangelist, prophet, teacher, friend, priest, parent, son or daughter, but we make the choice. Not every friend, not every teacher, not every father, not every priest can be such a person for us. But for the intellectual and spiritual "pulling together" of our lives such persons are very important.

Some mentors never know the role they have played in the lives of friends or strangers who have found them such an encouragement. Literary mentors, for example, play an integrating role for us. They become our soul mates because of a resonance we feel with their books and written thoughts. And we may feel this resonance even when we take strong exception to what they write at certain points. In fact, even in the exceptions we are able to collect and integrate our own journey and our own thinking.

This Book—a Mentor?

It may be presumptuous of me to think that I can write a book that would serve as a mentor for you who read it. But it is nonetheless just what the publishers have asked me to do.

"Earl," my editor said to me, "you have been involved with students at the University of California at Berkeley for over twenty years. You have seen them become Christians, mature and take their place in the church and in society at large. You have seen some of them falter, some fail and some succeed in amazing ways. Think about it. If you had a dozen or so main things you would like to say to Christians just becoming familiar with being an adult, what would they be?"

Well, I did think about it, and this book is the result. I want the chapters that follow not to appear as the sort of deadly advice that enervates the soul, that sets up goals only saints have ever reached, that, like a high-school graduation speech, places the burdens of the entire world on the fragile shoulders of youth. Rather I want these chapters to be *sheer encouragement*.

If I could, I would like to come alongside you, walk with you, listen to you, share with you something of my own journey, pass on the mentoring advice of my own mentors and add a bit of my own. Books often don't let that happen very well. But some in my library have done so marvelously. I hope this one does at least a little of this for you.

The Plan
In what follows I start at the beginning by passing on to you some of the best mentoring I have received—the challenge to stay close to Jesus. In this first section then follow reflections on Christian growth, Bible study, evangelism and lay ministry.

The second section takes up our relation as Christians to the surrounding world—reading to keep the mind alive, money, sex, and the great challenge of being peacemakers.

The final section turns specifically to our responsibility as Christians to give the sheer encouragement to our friends and family that will restore healthy relationships between us and serve as a model to the surrounding world. Christians are Christians twenty-four hours a day.

Section I

Staying Close to Jesus

Chapter 1

Staying Close to Jesus

When I first went off to theological seminary, I was warned about possible threats to my faith. I was warned about certain professors, about dangerous ideas and about becoming intellectually smug.

The same thing happened when I started my career as a pastor. I was warned about hypocrisy, clericalism, institutional irrelevancy, about fundamentalists who curtail freedom and liberals who dominate denominational committees. All the warnings were reasonable and partly valid. But they did me little good.

You see, warnings are like dried fruit: they have a long shelf life and a long aftertaste. The nourishment soon evaporates, but the bitter flavor stays on. Warnings create a generalized loss of appetite because of their own bad taste and because they make every future banquet for us suspect. We fear the possibility of contamination.

Our generation is "overwarned" by advisers who themselves have become disappointed and have decided that what each new generation needs is a few choice warnings to keep us on guard—rigid, frightened and off balance.

Staying Close to Jesus Christ

The best advice I received turned out to be relevant not only for my life as a seminary student and pastor but also as an ordinary Christian. A wise friend and pastor, a mentor, Dr. Richard Halverson, shared this with a small group of us. He was at that time pastor on the staff of Hollywood First Presbyterian Church. We were on our way to various theological schools.

His counsel was basic and without loopholes. "Stay close to Jesus Christ in your daily walk," he said simply. "Stay close to your brothers and sisters in Christ, trust the Holy Spirit to be your guide and companion, and jump right into the experience of being a student."

I have thought a lot about Dr. Halverson's advice, and I know now that he was really describing spirituality in its most fundamental form. Spirituality is not exotic "spiritual" giftedness, but it is just this: a day-to-day walk with Jesus Christ as Savior, Lord and friend; a day-to-day fellowship with God's people; the assurance within our hearts and minds that this is all we need to be spiritual; and then a discipleship attitude that jumps right into the daily challenge.

It is this spirituality I want to think about. Some of us almost lose our sanity trying to be spiritual. Others of us are lost in the pressures of student life, of professions, of work, of programs now gone obsessive and oppressive. We are losing our appetite for God. More than anything else each of us needs a simple, uncomplicated spirituality. If all this is true, why do we have so much trouble keeping our daily lives spiritually healthy? Let me suggest five reasons.

Spending Time with Jesus
First, spirituality in the Bible is fundamentally a relationship between Christians and the Lord Jesus Christ. The New Testament phrases "in Christ," "in the Spirit," "Christ in you," prove the point. Relationships take quality time. And most lack of spirituality is not, in my opinion, an infection of faith by diseased, false doctrine. It is more often the malnutrition and sluggishness that comes from a Christian starving for time with our living Lord in prayer and worship and Bible study.

If this is true, then the restoration of health will happen quickly and noticeably in direct proportion to our change in time priorities. A simple move on our part to focus our daily lives toward Jesus Christ will have immediate impact in favor of spiritual health.

Sound Doctrine
Second, there can, of course, be spiritually destructive infections that are more serious than the sluggishness I have just described. Bad doctrine can confuse and cause a spiritually cluttered life. In some instances, the very techniques and strategies for spirituality may be essentially unhealthy. There are Christians who are drawn away from a simple reliance on Jesus Christ, drawn away from simple relationships with Christian brothers and sisters by the very attempts they carefully and consciously make to become more spiritual. In place of a robust relationship with Jesus Christ and his people through the Holy Spirit, some "spiritual" programs substitute for simple, biblically rooted faith, spiritual self-righteousness and what amounts to impudent demands upon God.

The cure of such sickness is as uncomplicated as the process of the sickness is elaborate. It is the rediscovery of the gospel of Jesus Christ and the rediscovery of the ordinary Christians we are privileged to know because of the gospel. One theologian friend of mine told me that after he had studied several of the exotic spiritual movements of European and American Christianity with their "spiritual" success stories and their disdain for what they called nominal Christians, he found himself praying "Lord, make me a nominal Christian." He wanted more than ever to be an ordinary believer who simply trusts in the gospel of Jesus Christ on a day-by-day basis. He wanted to be centered upon Christ and nothing else.

Jumping into the Task at Hand

Third, another hindrance to spirituality is that we often withdraw into a private moment while we wait for something spiritually profound to happen. All the while we should have been jumping right into the everyday way of discipleship. We should have been working hard at the tasks that challenge our daily life.

Spirituality needs the private moment of personal prayer and meditation, but it also needs the open road of service and ministry, the banquet with the other brothers and sisters, and the hard interpersonal work places where testing can happen.

Spirituality describes a rhythmic, balanced life of work and rest, time alone and time with people, quiet time and adventurous discipleship activity. Spirituality means jumping into the task at hand. This is one of the reasons that Bible study shared with coworkers is so exciting.

Spirituality an Amateur Affair

Fourth, many of us have the mistaken notion that experts must teach us the deeper secrets of spirituality. But these spiritual giants and the communities that are created around them often turn us into religious groupies. Too much advice and too many religious procedures can make us victims of religious indigestion. The basic error is this: spirituality is understood as something "religious." But spirituality is not religion highly refined and polished. Spirituality is amateur and nonprofessional to the core.

The most spiritual moment in the lad Diggory's life in C. S. Lewis's *Magician's Nephew* is not while he is speculating about magic rings and magic bells but in that one awful moment when he blurts out to Aslan, the great Golden Lion, the deep worries of his heart and then dares to look squarely into Aslan's face, "But please, please—won't you—can't you give me something that will cure Mother?"

The spiritual summit of that story is reached just at the point when Diggory sees the great tear in Aslan's eye, and comes to know that his prayer, as stumbling and inadequate as it seemed to him, has been answered. He now knows that Aslan loves his mother just as Diggory does, perhaps even more.

The Most Spiritual and the Least Aware

Fifth and finally, I have an odd observation to make about my own experience of spiritual people: The ones who are most spiritual are least aware of it. This means that any one of us may be more spiritual than we realize we are.

In the New Testament, spiritual gifts are observed by others not by the self. Luke said of Barnabas that he was "a good man, full of the Holy Spirit" (Acts 11:24). Barnabas does not say it of himself.

Some of you feel inadequate precisely because your heart yearns for more time with Jesus Christ and more fellowship with his people, more time for worship and study of the Holy Scriptures. You may well have that feeling because you are healthy, not because you are sick. It has always been true that appetite is not a sign of illness but of health. So my advice is not for more strategies to make you spiritual. You already are! My advice is to jump right in as a student, as a pastor, as a Christian person. You have already had all the advice you need.

Chapter 2

The 24-Hour Christian

While I was serving as minister to students at University Presbyterian Church in Seattle, a student who called himself an atheist came to talk with me. Once in the middle of our conversation, he interrupted his own argument abruptly.

"I can't get Jesus Christ out of my mind," he said. "If I dismiss him as an idea he haunts me as a person. If I dismiss him as a person he haunts me as an idea."

Jesus Christ: Event and Word
An atheist should have no trouble getting Jesus the Messiah out of his mind. But this young man's atheism was obviously being challenged. New facts he was discovering from a small group Bible study in his university dorm were causing him to nego-

tiate his earlier certainty. This student was in the middle of making the greatest of all discoveries—the discovery of Jesus Christ. Many an unwary atheist is snared in just such a way.

He had already rightly recognized the basic philosophical issue: the fact that Jesus is both a person and a meaning. Jesus Christ is the event and he is the word. This means that if this student were to become a believer, he would both trust in the person of Jesus and in the truth of the good news about him. Both of his haunting intuitions would be fulfilled. He would know Christ as a friend: "I have called you friends" (Jn 15:15). And he would experience the meaning of life breaking into his own life: "I am the light of the world; he who follows me will not walk in darkness, but will have the light of life" (Jn 8:12). He would experience the great mystery of the good news: we as ordinary human beings are welcomed into the fellowship with the very source of all truth.

This news is good because ultimate truth is tenaciously personal. Jesus Christ is the Word of Truth in the mystery of his eternal nature and yet he is knowable as the living Lord.

When we trust in Christ, the negotiation of all values is inevitable. We will weigh the journey of our life thus far. "I am the door; if any one enters by me, he will be saved, and will go in and out and find pasture. . . . I came that they may have life, and have it abundantly" (Jn 10:9-10). In finding Jesus Christ we are now invited by Christ to gather together all that we are and know of ourself and bring our total selfhood through the shepherd-door himself.

Maturity, Peter Pan and Jesus Christ
What do I find as I do this weighing? I find that Jesus Christ makes sense of all the rest of my life. He draws together every part of my experience just like all the great themes of the history of Israel converge in Jesus Christ. The older part of the

journey by itself is incomplete because by its very nature it points forward—beyond itself and its own limitations.

We understand this from our own journey. First we are children in a family. All of the tradition that goes with childhood is meaningful in itself, but it is also a preliminary part of the total human journey. Childhood prepares for youth and youth for maturity. No one can remain a child in an ideal child-family or child-peer world of permanent pre-adolescence or permanent adolescence.

Nevertheless we like Peter Pan. Why is this so? Precisely because we are unlike him: we grow up. Though our wistfulness about childhood joy creates Peter Pan, most of the time we actually want to mature. In fact for most children, contrary to Peter Pan, it is the reality of growing up that gives the special joy to childhood:

"How tall you are growing."

"What did you learn in school today?"

"Look at me, Mom. I can swim five laps now!"

"I watched Sis at dance class, and I said to myself, 'I can do that.' "

There would be no joy in childhood were we forced to remain a child permanently while all our companions grew taller, more skillful in sports and wiser in thought. The earlier time of our own life, just like the past time of human history, looks forward toward resolution and fulfillment. The Law of Moses by its nature stirs up our respect for the giver of such a Law and by its nature points toward its completion.

In the same way the former part of our own journey has its own meanings that must be completed. It is an exciting list that tells our story: birth, families, individuality, hopes, traditions. It is a tragic list too: death, frustrated plans, family breakup, disappointments.

The big questions of human existence are these: How is such

a resolution for my journey and the journey of history to be found? The boldness of the promise Jesus made is now all the more clear to us. "I am the door, if any one enters by me he will find. . . ." Jesus Christ makes the bold claim that he is able to resolve the whole story of our lives.

The Mirror of the Law

The Law of Moses is completely true, and yet it is the tragedy of the Law that it cannot heal the crisis it inevitably reveals. The Law is like the magic mirror in *Snow White:* it tells the truth unfailingly. When the queen asks, "Who is the fairest of them all?" she hears from the mirror what she does not want to hear. But there is nothing further that the mirror is able to do; it has told the truth. So the queen becomes wicked and tries to suppress the truth through murder and intrigue.

So the Law mirrors the truth to us. But what do we do with truth it tells? What do we do when the truth is hard to welcome? We would like to be complete, but we feel incomplete and we look for some sign of hope.

This profound incompleteness is evident in the Old Testament itself, especially in ancient Israel's ceremonies that seek forgiveness from God. The blood of an animal is sprinkled ceremonially, but the people have no real relationship with the animal that is sacrificed by the priests. We witness a religious enactment, and, even while we watch such a rite as Yom Kippur (The Day of Atonement), we sense its enormous inadequacy. We sense that such a ceremony must somehow point beyond itself toward a greater Shepherd-Lamb who was yet to come. Jesus is that greater Shepherd-Lamb: "I know my own and my own know me, . . . and I lay down my life for the sheep" (Jn 10:15).

Like a trustworthy guide, the Law is sheer truth; it portrays the grand design. Then as an accuser the Law brings me to the

Shepherd-Lamb who takes my place so that sin and death may be disarmed. He is the Lamb I am related to; I can know him and love him. He is not a victim of a ceremony because he knows the meaning of all that is taking place at the cross.

Jesus: the Center of History, the Center of Our Life

The story of our lives is not unlike the story of the Old Testament people. The mixtures of good and bad, of hopes and failures, of rich traditions and half-told stories converge at the doorway of the Shepherd-Lamb. Jesus Christ is the one who makes our joys complete because he both endorses our hopes and resolves our profound crises. In Christ we discover that it is God's will to bless us. The hints of this fulfillment of our destiny were there all the time in Israel's prophecies and songs, just as they were scattered through the older part of our own history.

Jesus Christ is the Lord of reconciliation, and therefore our crisis of failures and profound need does not leave him disarmed. He is able to cope with "our mistakes just as he can cope with what we imagine to be our good deeds," said Dietrich Bonhoeffer.

As we trust in Jesus Christ we invite him to become our Shepherd-Lamb, and we become his disciples, his followers, his learners.

But what is it that we are to learn? The disciples in the New Testament followed Jesus and learned about him. They learned how Christ fulfills life by setting his disciples free from the dominating terror of sin and death. If we are disciples in the twentieth century, we will learn the same things that they did. We too will learn how Christ sets us free to reach our full stride as human beings. We too will learn the meaning of forgiveness and the mystery of the victory over death.

Who but Jesus Christ is the convergence point where the

profoundest expectations and the profoundest crises of all history come together in the one historical time, in this one concrete place, in one unique person? If we do not trust in Jesus Christ as this Shepherd-Door through whom we will bring the whole mixture of who we are, then the overwhelming question we must answer is this: What or whom shall we propose to put in his place? Who or what will be able to draw together the vast numbers of theme threads that make up our lives?

Jesus Christ: The Grand Middle Place
Faith first happens when I decide to trust in Jesus Christ—and faith stays healthy and growing as I daily decide to stay close to Jesus Christ throughout the whole journey.

Here we stand at the middle of everything. What is both profound and exciting is that we never outgrow this grand middle place. We never progress beyond Jesus Christ. There is no greater spiritual or intellectual or mystical breakthrough that awaits us further on along the way. In Christ is enough abundance to last a lifetime. As his disciples we spend our lifetime growing in the mystery of who Jesus Christ is and in working out the full possibilities of his will for our lives.

Grace and the Sleeping Christian
I am grateful that there were mentors in my student years who pointed me toward this vital center and gave me the good advice: "Stay close to Jesus Christ." Karl Barth, who has become for me a formative literary mentor, put it this way:

Christology is the touchstone of all knowledge of God in the Christian sense. . . . "Tell me how it stands with your Christology, and I shall tell you who you are." . . . Look! This is the point now! Either knowledge, or the greatest folly. . . . The world was lost, but Christ was born, rejoice.

Have you ever thought of this question? Are you a disciple

when you are asleep or only when you are awake? The answer is not as simple as it appears. For me this issue first arose during a discussion my senior year at Princeton Seminary. We were trying to answer the question "Who is a Christian?" and our answers were very brave and inspiring. We had agreed that a Christian is someone who really believes in Jesus Christ, one who has the courage to be, one who is concerned prophetically for justice because of grace, and . . . (the list continued with various special marks of the Christian that student after student would add to the profile).

Then someone commented. "Your Christian," he said, "is by definition only a Christian when he or she is awake and able to believe, care, grow in ethical implication, and so forth. What happens when your Christian is asleep?" That question forced me to realize that every definition of discipleship must finally have in it as much of God's grace as it has of our faith.

It is Jesus Christ who makes us Christians, and that great fact of grace preserves our freedom and keeps us safe through the times when we are not able to decide because we are asleep or otherwise helpless. The good news is more than the good news of our faith. It is the good news of Jesus Christ who is not helpless. This is the wondrous mystery of Christian discipleship. It is by faith that we decide, and nothing must blur the importance of our lifelong deciding, which is what faith is all about. But God decides too, and his decision born out of grace keeps us throughout our lives.

When we choose to trust in Jesus Christ, we stay close to him. And he stays close to us.

Chapter 3

Up from Mount Shasta

I have already dropped a few hints about my own spiritual background and something of the mentors in my own life. I will continue to do that in the chapters that follow. Still it may be helpful to you to know a bit more about how I came to faith in Jesus Christ and, as well, how I found myself being drawn more and more to a direct Christian ministry with students.

From Shasta to Berkeley

I am a third-generation Californian, and I was brought up near Mount Shasta. My family was wonderful—free-wheeling, enthusiastic, encouraging—but not particularly religious. I stopped attending church toward the end of high school and refrained from attending during my first two years at the University of California at Berkeley. Church just was not part of my life.

During my sophomore year at Cal, I lived in Barrington Hall, which was then and still is an outlandish place. About 250 men lived in Barrington Hall at that time.

Bible Study—Barrington Style

In the middle of my sophomore year a friend invited me to a Bible study group. A few students were meeting once a week in a student's room to study a book from the New Testament; it was that simple. They met for about an hour to discuss a New Testament book.

I still remember my first impression. I was shocked to see young men my own age reading the New Testament through adult eyes and talking about it seriously. It was a stunning experience.

I didn't have a Bible then (though we did have Bibles at home), so I had to look on with somebody else. I was so impressed that I said, "I want to keep coming to this Bible study group." So that week I bought a Bible. Not knowing the different translations, I ended up buying a King James. When I went back to the study group the following week, they said, "We're not using that Bible; we're using the RSV." So I had to buy another Bible. There I was, not even a Christian yet, and I had already bought two Bibles in one week.

Trusting the Trustworthiness of Christ

That spring I started to attend the college group at the First Presbyterian Church of Berkeley, and in the summer I went to a conference at Lake Tahoe where the two speakers were Edward John Carnell from Fuller Theological Seminary and Robert Boyd Munger, the pastor of First Pres.

I will always remember the turning point in my life when, at that conference, Bob Munger posed the issue. He said, "When you are convinced of the trustworthiness of Jesus Christ so that you are willing to trust in his trustworthiness, then you are ready to become a Christian." He said it to the group as a whole, but I felt he was speaking directly to me. I can remember going down to the lake and deciding that I wanted to trust in the trustworthiness of Jesus Christ.

This took place at the beginning of my junior year. When I returned to Berkeley, I rose fast. I had become more involved in the Barrington Bible study group and finally became president of Barrington Hall, as well as president of the college group at First Presbyterian.

Amazing things happened toward the end of my senior year at Cal. We saw men in that hall, almost one a week toward the end, becoming Christians. It just happened, one way or another. They came out of the woodwork, and the Lord honored that ministry.

From Berkeley to Princeton

In the middle of my senior year, although I was a pre-law/political science major, I was so turned on by what was happening in that Bible study group and by having chances to witness as a Christian that I said to my pastor, Bob Munger, "You know, this is what really turns me on. I wonder if I should be a minister."

"Why don't you apply to Princeton Seminary and see?" he replied.

So I did, and I was accepted, probably the rawest, greenest recruit they ever had.

First Pres. in Berkeley arranged for me to have Lynn Boliek, a staunch Calvinist, as my roommate. He helped me a great deal in my first year at Princeton. Others who were worried sick that I would be lost to liberalism made sure that I went to a Navigator conference at Star Ranch before I went to Princeton.

I made all kinds of discoveries that were theologically important to me. I also discovered John A. Mackay, the greatest preacher that I had ever heard. I had three great years at Princeton and then went into my ministry. But what had first happened to me at Barrington Hall in Berkeley left an indelible mark.

At Princeton in those days all seminarians were supposed to go out in gospel teams, which I did not really enjoy. It wasn't my thing to go out to churches and read the Scripture in worship services, and then talk to the youth and be farmed out to families for lunch. We were representing the Seminary and we were doing good, of course, more or less.

Bible Study—Princeton Style

But the next-to-last time I went out, it was to Jenkintown outside of Philadelphia. I had lunch with the Kelly family. There was a young son in that family named Glenn, a freshman at Princeton University, who happened to be home at the time. Talk about divine appointments—I really believe in them.

"Oh, you're from Princeton University," I said. "I'm from Princeton Seminary. How interesting! We ought to get together up there."

He said, "Great." So the next week we got together and I told him. "You know, Glenn, when I was at Berkeley I got involved with a small Bible study group, and it really meant a lot to me. I don't have one of those here at Princeton. Do you think you guys might be interested in one?"

He said, "I'll ask my roommate." So that started off a little Bible study group at Princeton.

I ended up involved with about seven of those groups at one time, because other groups began to ask me to help them out.

That was my ministry throughout my three years at Princeton. The groups met at either 10 P.M., 6 A.M. or 4:30 P.M. They were always about one hour long, and I used the Barrington format, a simple quasi-inductive method of studying together different books in the New Testament. Some weeks the apostle Paul won and some weeks he lost. But I didn't worry about that. I simply tried to look at the text with the other students and to help them understand what was there. I discovered the same thing here as in Berkeley. Given time, if I could get somebody to look at the text, it would sooner or later win their respect.

Investigative Bible Study

Investigative Bible Study Groups is what I called them. I don't like the term "Evangelistic Study Groups." Why carry special baggage to Bible study? Let's just study the text because it deserves to be studied and let God do the evangelizing if he chooses. Today in northern California, InterVarsity calls those Bible studies Investigative Bible Study Groups.

Several young men at Princeton became Christians in those groups. I never put any pressure on them or made any great move to try to get them to become Christians; it just happened. In a basic way this discovery shaped my whole style of ministry as well as my theological method. My ministry in Seattle, in Manila and in Berkeley has been founded on this basic premise; if I can get people to consider the text seriously, it will do its own convincing.

From Bible to Ethics

That principle has taken much pressure off me. I haven't had to try to be clever or have elaborate programs. Although it has sometimes taken some skill, what I have needed to do most of all is to get people to consider the text. I became convinced that the best theology and the most substantial ethics always begin with the text. It is not a matter of taking the world-questions and then trying to see if we can find something in the Bible to speak to the world, but rather of drawing our ethics from the text and then confronting the world.

In his remarkable two-volume work, *Theological Ethics,* Helmut Thielicke draws the distinction between the theologies of Paul Tillich and Karl Barth, and he used this basic approach in contrasting the two theological methods. He points out that Paul Tillich, whose main concern was "correlation," begins with the categories of the world. That is why his theology is basically existential and speculative. He begins with the categories of the world, and then asks questions of existence and moves toward their theological implications. Thielicke points out that, in contrast, Karl Barth begins with the text and moves toward the world to see where the collision occurs.

He uses as an example of this theological modeling the Barmen Declaration of 1934 written primarily by Karl Barth. Each of the six articles begins with a text and moves from the text toward the world. For example, Article 1 begins with John 14: "I am the Way, the Truth, and the Life; no one comes to the Father but by me." Then comes the article: "Jesus Christ, as he is attested for us in Holy Scripture, is the one word of God which we have to hear and which we have to trust and obey in life and in death." And then the negation: "We reject the false doctrine, as though the church could and would have to acknowledge as a source of its proclamation, apart from and besides this one word of God, still other events and powers, figures, and truths, as God's revelation."

Notice that Barth started with the text, moved toward the Nazi Germany of 1934, and then the collision becomes obvious and concrete. He did not start with the existential setting and then try to speculate possible correlations. In other words, he began as a biblical theologian. Barth as the theologian took the same journey: He began with his *Der Römerbrief,* his commentary on Romans, then went on to systematic theology.

Theologically and ethically from my own experience with these Bible study groups as well as my own theological formation in seminary I became convinced that I wanted to be a biblical Christian—an angular biblical theologian rather than a smoothly synchronized theologian.

It is against this backdrop that I write the present book and, in the following chapter, speak about the role of Bible study in a growing Christian's life.

Learning God's Mind

What is a biblical Christian? Surely it is someone who wants to live his or her discipleship under the text.

As a biblical Christian I will want to understand what the Old and New Testaments say and what they mean. My experience with Bible study at Berkeley and Princeton will not be enough. I will need to stay involved in Bible study throughout my whole life. I will need the fellowship of other Christians to help me fully understand the intent and meanings of the words I read.

For this reason I will need a fellowship that is historically rooted, one which is aware of the past, one which acknowledges the understandings of Christians who lived their lives in a time different from my own. This is where the Barmen Declaration and other great confessions of the church come in.

They keep our interpretations from being only private. For Christian faith is personal but not private.

Most of all I will need the illumination of the Holy Spirit. His illumination and confirmation of God's Word is the mysterious element that accompanies Bible study when the Jesus Christ who is portrayed to me in the Old and New Testaments wins my respect and draws me toward his character. The Jesus Christ of the biblical witness, in the Old Testament by anticipation and in the New Testament by witness, is the one who wins my faith. Then, in borrowed fashion, the document that surrounds him grows in authority because of its Living Center.

Jesus Christ: The Living Center
The Bible's authority over my life is derived from this Living Center, Jesus Christ the Lord.

All doctrines gain their authoritative importance by their relative proximity to Christ and their fulfillment in Christ. Thus in the yearnings of the Psalms in the Old Testament we see Jesus Christ who is their fulfillment. When our Lord Jesus Christ quoted the opening of Psalm 22 as he died on the cross, he fulfilled not only the opening lines of anguish but, in the resurrection and spread of the gospel, the closing paean of praise, as well. We see Christ also in the Law and in the history of the people of Israel. One way or another they bring us to Jesus Christ.

When my faith is rooted in daily study of the Bible, I not only benefit spiritually and ethically but I am set free from the unhealthy domination of political, social and religious fads and leaders.

The Bible grants a framework that is focused toward its center. And just as every theme in its pages focuses on Jesus Christ, I learn to focus my daily life on him. We do not idolize or worship the Bible. In fact the Bible itself prohibits such idolatry.

We worship the Lord of the Bible who is the Living Word to which the real people who wrote the Bible bear witness.

Staying a biblical Christian takes work just as any substantial growth in my spiritual life takes work, but the rewards are worth it.

The Source of Authority: The Bible or Experience?

Staying a biblical Christian has far-reaching consequences. When someone asks me to talk about my Christian faith or to explain what the gospel is at an InterVarsity campus meeting or a Young Life weekend retreat, what do I say? What is the source for such teaching?

To put the question in theological perspective: What is the authority for the message of a pastor, or Young Life leader at a Tuesday evening club meeting, or a seminary professor lecturing on the Third Article of the Apostle's Creed; or for any Christian who seeks to understand and share the meaning of the Christian gospel?

The answer is not as simple as we might suppose! Consider this possibility: Let's say that as a Christian I have just experienced with new and fresh reality the full impact of God's grace. My experience is dramatically real and immediate. I have no doubt that the experience is a gift from God. My attitudes and my lifestyle have changed. I am confident that it's God's work.

Shall I not preach this experience? Isn't this very immediate and thrilling story the message I should as a pastor affirm on Sunday morning or Tuesday evening? Isn't this contemporary work of the Holy Spirit in the lives of God's people the most relevant message for our time? Especially since it is my experience!

Or add a further possibility: What of the even greater spiritual breakthroughs that some Christians have experienced—

visions, dreams, angels? Many would insist that these gifts of the Holy Spirit deserve to be affirmed and proclaimed so that the world may be humbled by such signs and the Christians encouraged. What should be our reply?

For visions and for all of the experiences of God's grace we are grateful, but they are neither our message nor the source of our message. We do not proclaim them as if they were the good news. Rather we must proclaim the gospel of Jesus Christ. The Jesus Christ we preach is the historical Jesus, and the only authoritative witness to that gospel is the Bible. This means that the authority for the church is not the church, not the existential experiences of signs and wonders experienced by Christians, not the challenging new visions of spiritual leaders, not the revolutionary imperatives of this new historical era, not the safe status quo priorities of the present social majority.

The warm and personal endorsement of the good news that comes from our own experiences of the love of God are important twentieth-century witnesses to the timelessness of the reign of Christ, but they lack any binding authority in themselves. As good as they are, they are not the message.

In an ironic sense the same observation may be made of the moral tragedies of life, the profound failures that are the result of human sin. These also are twentieth-century signposts which cry out the need of humanity, and they demand a salvation that only Jesus Christ grants. But neither the positive experiences of the faithful, nor the negative rejection of a world alienated and confused, have in themselves any binding authority over life. They are not the content of the message.

No New Doctrines
For this reason we must reject as false any doctrine which teaches that the Holy Spirit continues to reveal new authoritative doctrines to the church beyond the fulfillment of all reve-

lation—Jesus Christ the Lord. Jesus promised: "The Holy Spirit, whom the Father will send in my name, he will teach you all things, and bring to your remembrance all that I have said to you" (Jn 14:26).

Paul prescribes precisely the same testing principle for the Colossian Christians. He tells us that every doctrine must be tested by its relationship to the true center, which is God's speech once and for all in Jesus Christ (Col 2). This means that we have a criterion for the testing of all doctrine.

The early church, by its agreement on the canon of Holy Scripture, interpreted Paul's testing principle as follows: All doctrine must be tested by its submission to the historical witness that surrounds Jesus Christ, namely, the Bible, consisting of the Old Testament and the New Testament. As we trust in Jesus Christ, we trust in the witness to him. We have been convinced by the Holy Spirit of the Jesus Christ we have met in the biblical witness to him.

John Calvin put it this way in his discussion of the doctrine of the Holy Spirit: "The whole of it comes to this: the Holy Spirit is the bond by which Christ binds us to Himself." The church's doctrine of the inspiration of the Scriptures rests on the belief that the Holy Spirit has preserved the faithfulness and trustworthiness of the documents and that the Holy Scriptures are those books God wants us to have. They point us faithfully to the center.

The Total Sufficiency of Jesus Christ

The Bible derives its authority in the following fashion. Because the historic Jesus of Nazareth is the only Redeemer and the good news is complete in him, there are therefore no hidden new gospels to be found or revealed. This conviction of the total sufficiency of Jesus Christ underlies the meaning of the doctrine of the infallibility of the Bible. By that doctrine we agree that only one word has been spoken—Jesus Christ himself. He alone shall have final binding authority over our lives and doctrines.

Every new doctrinal statement, therefore, must be tested by the biblical witness. Every Christian doctrine should itself begin with its own willingness to be tested.

The Barmen Declaration of the German Confessing Church of 1934 opened in just such a way: "Try the spirits whether they are of God! Prove also the words of the Confessional Synod of the German Evangelical Church to see whether they agree with Holy Scripture and with the Confessions of the Fathers. If you find that we are speaking contrary to Scripture, then do not listen to us! But if you find that we are taking our stand upon Scripture, then let no fear or temptation keep you from treading with us the path of faith and obedience to the Word of God, in order that God's people be of one mind upon earth and that we in faith experience what he himself has said: 'I will never leave you, nor forsake you.' Therefore, 'Fear not, little flock, for it is your Father's good pleasure to give you the kingdom.' "

A Defense against Visions

Christians through the centuries have discovered that such confidence in the Bible results in our greatest freedom from bondage to the false and the exotic. If we are not clear about this fundamental confidence, we shall be easily victimized throughout our lives by the visions and dreams of powerful and persuasive people around us. Apart from this standard for testing doctrines, we have no defense against their visions—or, for that matter, our own visions.

Those who build their teaching upon spiritual breakthroughs claim so much and try so hard to convince us that this teaching is more relevant because the vision or experience is more recent than older truth. Moreover, they may support the new spiritual breakthrough with dramatic illustrations of power—and we remember from historical experience that public support quickly gathers around any proof of power. Political tyrants always use both the army and the arena, the power of the sword and of the circus. Religious tyrants also have learned the importance of power.

How are we to answer the claims that now become the underpinnings of whole new schemes and elaborate doctrines? I believe that over the long pull the best corrective in the face of error is the positive affirmation of the truth. Add to that the demonstration of what Francis Schaeffer calls the "mark of the Christian"—the love of Christ at work through us toward others. Jesus Christ is the one who finally proves substantial when the exotic movements have crumbled. The text of the Scriptures makes more sense in the long run when exotic themes have begun to collapse in upon themselves.

Loyalty to the Bible

What then constitutes loyalty to the biblical witness in the teaching and preaching mandate of the church? Confusion over this question has been created by the fact that most Christian churches and most quasi-Christian movements as well claim some degree of loyalty to the Bible.

Our search for a clear answer brings us to the important role of biblical and theological study in the life of the Christian and the church. The vigorous practice of theology and biblical exegesis (the accurate rendering of the essential content of a text) is vital for the health of the church in the world today.

What does the text actually say (exegesis)?

What does it mean and how does the individual part of the biblical teaching fit with the whole (biblical theology)?

Then finally, what are the overall themes and conclusions that we may draw together in order to form the basis of affirming our faith to the world (systematic theology)?

At each step of the way, the testing process at work among ordinary Christians should always be encouraged. Our work and our conclusions must not be absolutized. The only absolute in Christian faith is God himself and his Speech. Our faith, our affirmations, even our doctrines about the Bible are not absolute, nor do our theological conclusions have final binding authority. Every Christian must always question every doctrine: What is the evidence? Not of my feelings, nor of the popular folk preference, nor of the historical appearances around us— but what is the evidence of the biblical texts themselves?

The principle here, it seems to me, is that a Christian is prepared to order faith and life on the basis of the gospel. Biblical Christianity has Jesus Christ as center. What matters here is the daily walk of the Christian man and woman with Christ by faith. Prayer, simple obedience, confession of our sins and acceptance of our belovedness are the ingredients of the Christian life into which the Bible invites us to enter and enjoy. As a result of the personal relationship with the living Christ and the supportive ministry of the Holy Spirit, the biblical witness draws us into the mandates of the way of discipleship in the world.

When it comes to the content of faith, the question that the biblical Christian submits to is this: "If I can be shown that the Bible teaches a doctrine, I will believe it." That is, as I see it, the real issue, not how gloriously a Christian speaks *about* the Bible. But more to the point than the superlatives used to describe its wonder is simply this: Are we prepared to order the way we live and believe on the basis of the Bible's teaching?

Clarity of the Biblical Portrait

Here we must consider some criteria for the use of Scripture in our relationships within the church. As we test our doctrines with one another, some themes become very clear and definite; others are less clear and, therefore, we are able to be less definite in our advocacy of them. For some doctrines there is strong textual evidence which encourages us to endorse them boldly, while others with less such evidence should be advocated with more modest restraint.

For example, we preach many more sermons about the resurrection of Jesus Christ than about the one-sentence mention of baptism on behalf of the dead (1 Cor 15:29). The victory of Christ has clearly more authority for preaching and, therefore, we commend it heartily to those around us. But the one sentence about a baptism for the dead is too obscure in itself and in its setting for us to develop a strong doctrine for affirmation. We are not completely certain of what Paul means by his statement to the Christians in answer, perhaps, to a question they had put to him. Therefore, we dare not urge it upon the brothers and sisters in the church in the same way as we affirm the salvation we have in Jesus Christ. For the doctrine of Christ's resurrection there is much Bible teaching on the cross of Christ and his victory over death.

Where such problems of interpretation occur, either because of a scarcity of textual evidence or because of the presence of different teachings upon a theme, the biblical Christian must show restraint proportionate to the clarity of the whole biblical portrait. We must learn how to discover the relative biblical weight of a particular theme by relating each doctrinal concept we meet to those greater themes which the Bible floods with evidence and confirmation.

The first great theologian in the pages of the Gospels is John the Baptist. In John 3:22-36, in a dialog between John and members of the Pharisaic party, we have an example of his theological method. Every Christian is drawn into similar encounters in which a distinctive feature or theological emphasis with which we are identified is a point of debate.

In this discussion about baptisms and rites of purification John the Baptist proves to be as wise a theologian as he is daring as a prophet. He looks for the larger context within which the smaller theme of "baptism and rites of purification" may be helpfully considered. It is clear from the dialog recorded for us that John the Baptist realizes that the real question is not the rite of baptism but the mighty act of God himself in Jesus Christ to which every other theme must receive its own true meaning and weight. John points directly and unambiguously toward Jesus Christ as the true resolution of the questions raised by all "washings."

A conversation with my children a few years ago illustrates the point. Our then ten-year-old son, Jon, asked the question: "Dad, how does a cassette recorder work?

Our daughter Elizabeth, then age six, quickly jumped in to answer, "You press this button at the top."

Jon seemed unimpressed, so she tried again: "Look, Jon, these two wheels turn like this."

Jon still declined her answer: "No, I know all that."

She still had answers: "Maybe you didn't push the right button."

His patience was wearing thin because it finally became clear that he didn't want information about which switches to turn (he knew that already). He wanted an answer to a deeper question—how the music of John Denver is electronically impressed on the tape. At this point it was Elizabeth who began to lose interest.

Anne, our oldest daughter, was better able to carry on the conversation Jon had in mind.

The Larger Themes
The biblical Christian as theologian must continually move

with each question toward the deeper, larger themes. For this task we need each other—those who understand our questions and those who misunderstand. John the Baptist needed the intense questions of the Pharisees to help him clarify the larger issues. In the same way, we in our century are aided in our own theological clarification by the challenges that come to us from the world around us.

Speaking of his antagonist John Eck, Martin Luther said: "So, too, Eck provoked me. He made me wide awake. . . . Accordingly our opponents are very useful to us, although they think they do us harm."

A Twofold Humility
As we seek to understand the meaning of a doctrine, a twofold humility should characterize our approach. First, we should ask the Lord to be our leader in understanding the intent of Scripture. Second, we should ask for the check-and-balance help of our brothers and sisters in Christ—the church. The historic confessions of the church give guidance. So does the contemporary church.

Luther's Twin Principles of Biblical Interpretation
Martin Luther offered two rules that he followed in interpreting Holy Scripture: "First, if some passage is obscure I consider whether it treats of grace or of law, whether wrath or the forgiveness of sin (is contained in it) and with which of these it agrees better. By this procedure I have often understood the most obscure passages. . . . The second rule is that if the meaning is ambiguous I ask those who have a better knowledge of the language than I have whether the Hebrew/Greek words can bear this or that sense . . . and that is most fitting which is closest to the argument of the book."

Luther's two rules are essential. First, he looks for the larger context within which the particular teaching belongs. Second, he works hard to understand meanings of the words in their own language and usage, and what the text means when understood within its own textual setting.

A Timeless Witness

Biblical Christians are not bibliolaters. We worship Jesus Christ, not the Holy Bible. The Bible, taken seriously, never stimulates false worship, but by its texts and themes, its history and poetry, its yearnings and prayers, its real people from Moses to John, the Bible points us to the Lord. Therefore, when the Bible is truly authoritative for our faith, there is little danger of that faith becoming sidetracked with insignificant themes and cultic curiosities.

Because of the timelessness of Jesus Christ himself, the Bible's witness to his ministry is also timeless. The biblical Christian is not in bondage to the tyranny of the current, to the oppressive pressure of the "in" cause. The James party at Galatia must have panicked many Greek Christians with the "new word" that the truest Christians would not only believe in Christ but also would become Jewish. Paul employed the larger context of the gospel to apply to their claims, and out of that controversy his Letter to the Galatians became a declaration of independence for all Christians who have ever been browbeaten by the latest fad or movement. And in Acts 15 we have evidence that Paul's argument along with Barnabas also won over the respect of the leader of the Jewish Christians, James! As biblical Christians we are free from false gods because the Bible has bound us to the true God.

A Sharpened Sensitivity to the World around Us

Biblical faith does not blunt our ability to be shrewd observers of the contemporary scene. I believe the pressure of the gospel rather creates just the opposite effect—a sharpened sensitivity and inquisitiveness growing out of a stance toward life that does not need to fear truth wherever it is found. The Bible has committed to us the way of truth without equivocation. "Walk in the light, as he [God] is in the light" (1 Jn 1:7).

Theological Wanderlust
There is a doctrinal wanderlust that often takes hold of certain Christians. It tends to create its own momentum, and within it an insatiable appetite for the new and different for their own sake, an appetite for the novel. This wanderlust should not be confused with the research instinct that we have been describing, or the hard work of theological inquiry.

The restlessness in research is founded upon the principle of testing followed by meaningful response to truth discovered, whereas the restlessness of doctrinal wanderlust is dominated by inner moods, by the current immediate impression. Wanderlust is not freedom, though it disguises itself as freedom.

In the classic river scene in *Huckleberry Finn* it is the slave, Jim, who is in the truest sense free—not Huck—because Jim knows who he is, whereas Huck at that point in the story is simply a young boy adrift on the Mississippi. He must learn from Jim though he thinks of himself as the teacher.

An Exciting Task
I can think of no more exciting task in our age, so often adrift, and yet underneath it all so hungry for the real, than to have the privilege of sharing in the witness to Jesus Christ, the same yesterday, today and tomorrow. This is what being a biblical Christian is all about.

Chapter 5

Inevitable Surprise

I have been involved with students on the West Coast of the United States for a long time. For several of those years whenever I would meet students from an Oregon school I would ask if they knew Rebecca Manley (now Rebecca Manley Pippert, author of *Out of the Saltshaker*). During those years Becky was a campus staff member for InterVarsity Christian Fellowship working on Oregon campuses. I met many students who not only knew her but told me stories of how in one way or another through her influence they had become Christians. She had warmly introduced them to Jesus Christ in a way they could understand.

One day I told Becky that from my experience with the students I was meeting I had concluded that she was an evangelist among university students, and a remarkable one at that. Her response seemed more remarkable. She was surprised by what I said and told me that she had no particular evangelistic strategy, but that the results must have been due to her relationships with students and the Bible studies she was leading and encouraging. She was really quite shocked that so many students looked to her influence as having been decisive.

Later it dawned on me. Of course! That is just the point. Evangelism should be a surprise—especially to the evangelist—because it happens with people we meet when we are being who we are and sharing what God has given to and through us. In short, it happens when we are staying close to Jesus.

Evangelism is a long word for a simple, Christian mandate. It is a good mandate because the very word points to its source—the *good news* about the love and faithfulness of Jesus Christ. Because it is the Lord who hands out this mandate, every Christian is an evangelist.

This good news has become ours to share with other people. But first it is ours to experience. We discover in our own lives the forgiveness and new life in Jesus Christ. Then it is ours to share. Indeed, the power at the core of Jesus' love for us becomes the enabling authority and the motivation for every sharing ministry in the world. We are evangelists when we invite other people to trust in the Lord Jesus Christ as their Savior and Lord just as we have.

When I think of the ministry of evangelism, four sets of opposites come to my mind. First, evangelism is natural and yet sometimes unnatural. Second, evangelism is personal and yet public. Third, evangelism is a thoughtful event that fully involves the mind and yet it is profoundly mysterious and beyond intellectual or spiritual figuring out. Finally, evangelism takes time because it is a journey, and yet it is immediate and whimsically instantaneous.

Natural and Unnatural

How is it possible for us to do things that are natural and unnatural at the same time? In the physical world, we are accustomed to such contrasts. We know that it is unnatural for a human being to exist at an elevation of 40,000 ft. and at temperatures of 70 degrees below zero Fahrenheit. Yet, by the skillful management of the natural physical laws of aerodynamics and by the creation of an artificial climate inside a 747 jet, we are able not only to exist at 40,000 ft. above sea level but to watch movies and even phone home to let the folks know we will be forty-five minutes late because of head winds. There we are—living naturally in an unnatural place.

But what about the spiritual journey? Can the natural and unnatural dwell so easily together in that setting? Sharing our faith and something as personal as our own discovery of God's grace can be natural for us, but it can become unnatural. We naturally want to invite other people to join us in the joyous breakthrough of Christ's love into human history for we ourselves have discovered its generosity. The word should go out· There is a celebration going on and everyone is invited!

The apostle John tells his friends that he and other Christians are inviting those who read his letter to come into the *koinonia*, the fellowship, because the life of God is there, and this life is so good he wants others to know so that their joy together may be complete (1 Jn 1:4). John naturally wants to see the joy expand. And so do we.

It is natural to share a promise that means so much us. It is natural that we share the joy we have discovered and then invite our neighbor to discover it too.

I can still remember the day in 1945 when the war was over. Everyone told everyone! Yet, each person had to grasp the fact for themselves. So with the gospel a war has been won, and we have the news of the victory. That news needs telling. Yet because the war has been waged in each person's heart, each person must respond for themselves.

It is precisely because that promise of victory is so personal that there can also be an unnatural aspect to evangelism. I know from my own individual spiritual journey that the decision to follow Jesus Christ was and is a decision that I and only I can make for my own life. I must not forget this fact when I am sharing my faith.

It is unnatural for one human being to stand too close to the private core of another human being. For that is where the most important decisions are made. Each of us decides alone. And so I must know how to step back before my evangelism becomes dangerously unnatural and captive to the forced persuasiveness of the artificial atmosphere of high-pressure salesmanship, something like a movie at 40,000 ft.

I am talking about my respect for the person who hears the gospel from me. When I cross that line of respect or carelessly disregard it, I have not only offended the dignity of my neighbor but I have also put in jeopardy the integrity of the gospel of Jesus Christ. One of the main marks of our Lord's encounter with people is his profound respect for them. Jesus does not violate our right to make critical choices for ourselves.

Remember the rich, young ruler in Mark 10:17-22. He asked Jesus, "Good Teacher, what must I do to inherit eternal life?"

When Jesus heard the man say that he had kept all the commandments, even from his youth, Jesus lovingly said to him, "You lack one thing; go, sell what you have, and give to the poor, and you will have treasure in heaven; and come, follow me."

Jesus allows that baffled and struggling young man to work through his own response to the invitation to leave wealth behind and "come follow me." Jesus preserves the integrity of that moment of decision. And so must we.

When we honor this personal space, then evangelism is neither manipulation nor the art of taking over the decision-making responsibility for another human being. Evangelism is the forthright sharing of the good news with the invitation that Philip made to Nathanael, "Come and see" and then decide for yourself (Jn 1:46). It is, therefore, the best evangelism that carefully observes and respects this natural-unnatural crossover line.

Personal and Public
Evangelism is both personal and public. We make our own choices, but those choices have inevitable public consequences. Even a secret disciple like Nicodemus cannot keep the secret permanently (Jn 3:1-15; 7:50; 19:39). In several different ways, the commitment we make to follow Jesus Christ has public consequences; and so evangelism can never successfully sidestep or downplay its public results.

When I trusted Christ as my Lord, my values changed, my goals changed and my interpersonal relationships changed. And that was only the beginning! When I decided in favor of Christ, I became a part of a fellowship of ordinary men and women who had themselves also decided for Christ or who were in the process of deciding. I was not sure then just where each of these newly found brothers and sisters were on their own individual journeys of discipleship. In fact I am still not sure how to gauge the maturity of a companion on the journey of faith.

The more I think about it, the more I'm glad the measuring line is hidden. It means I must simply take each person at face value and trust their words until the evidence of faith, hope and love, like fruit on a tree, becomes testable in the eating. That testing happens throughout the journey of discipleship and it is unavoidably a public matter for public record. The fellowship of Christians is not a spiritually secret *civitas platonica,* but it is real people in a real place who, as Karl Barth put it, sometimes stir up a "public uproar."

All of this means that we invite each man or woman into a profoundly personal and unique experience with Jesus Christ, and that relationship leads inevitably to fellowship other believers who have also been invited. Thus we walk together. "You belong to Christ; I belong to Christ; we belong to each other" (E. Stanley Jones).

It is all very personal and very public at the same time. This is how the world is changed for the better. This is how we become the "light of the world" (Mt 5:14).

Thoughtful and Mysterious

Evangelism is an event of the mind. We invite a person to think carefully through the claims of Jesus of Nazareth. Yet at that same moment the mystery of God's self-disclosure cannot be intellectually contained.

Our alliance with truth is unshakable because Jesus Christ is the truth. Ultimately then there are only advantages and no long-term dangers to a full intellectual openness in the search for truth. We should never encourage a person to shut down questions of the mind so that the heart might believe more easily. Our gospel is the good news of truth for the mind alive with thoughtful questions as much as it is the good news of love for the heart alive with hope.

Heart and mind go together in biblical faith. Some people, however, are mostly drawn to Christ by reasonable arguments that bring together the pieces of what has primarily been for them an intellectual quest for truth. Others are persuaded by the heart more than the mind because their puzzle has not so much been a quest for answers as a resolution of reasons that reason could never understand. For them "The heart has its reasons that reason cannot know" (Pascal).

In each case, however, it is the truth of the gospel that does the resolving so that a person who is searching, whether in heart or mind, becomes a believer who trusts in the trustworthiness of Jesus Christ, a trustworthiness that is founded on truth.

Still, the wonder of becoming a Christian can never be finally explained by either the reason of the mind or the reason of the heart. At the core of all Christian faith there is a mystery. The Holy Spirit is the one who confirms the gospel, that settles its vast truth into our hearts so that I am able to say that Jesus Christ is my Lord and that I trust his love. No amount of argument can ever of itself create this wondrous discovery.

While we are earnestly trying our best to make a sensible case for Christianity, we must never forget the mystery. We are witnesses, but the Holy Spirit is the Evangelist.

Gradual and Immediate

Evangelism takes time. This is why in my opinion thoughtful, time-taking, friendship evangelism is the best evangelism. Through all the years that I have been a Christian, it has been made clear to me that the best evangelism is not done out of desperate urgency. That reveals more uncertainty on the part of the evangelist than it does confidence in the credibility of his message.

Evangelism is founded on profound respect for the integrity of both the good news of Jesus Christ and the person who is considering his claims. Nor is it my responsibility to say all that needs to be said to rightly make a credible case for Christian faith. Instead my task is to be faithful at each step of the journey that it is my privilege to share with my neighbor. This means that I should take the long view in every relationship, trusting the Holy Spirit to complete the confirmation of the message, the conviction of the sinner and the assurance of forgiveness.

When this long roadway of commitment is the pattern that I really trust, then the surprise of the suddenness of faith will confront me on every turn in the way. People who I thought were a long way from resolution will let me know that their questions have been solved. They now know enough to trust in Christ. When this happens, we who are trying to be evangelists are amazed by the ways that God proves himself. Such surprise is one of the best parts of being a Christian. Whatever I did or did not do, the pieces of the puzzle came together—and a neighbor became a fellow traveler on the way of life.

When I look back on the process, everything fits together and I recognize a naturalness about it all. It makes sense, it is personal and also public. It took time to happen and it happened by surprise.

The surprise is the best part. God confirms himself, I am not ready for it, yet it happens!

C h a p t e r   6

People in Power

"Are you a pastor?"

"No, I'm just a layman."

I've heard many variations on this conversation, especially as the word *layman* has been replaced by *layperson.* In any case, it is time to think about what is going through our minds when we say, "just a layman." The word *laity* itself is very historic; it simply means "people" and therefore it includes us all.

All Christians are a part of the people of God, the *laos* of God. Some of them are especially ordained for teaching and pastoral tasks, but most of us are and will always be a part of the laity. We are the ones who do not work for the church or a Christian organization like InterVarsity Christian Fellowship, but we make the work of the church happen. We are the teachers, servers, leaders—workers who volunteer to make the fellowship of Christ's people real everywhere.

Making the Church Happen

When you are a lay volunteer, you make the church happen. You feed youth groups. You free the church financially to carry on ministry. You make up committees that hire and fire church workers and set policy goals for the congregation. You teach Sunday-school classes and lead home Bible studies. You reach out to your neighborhoods and toward fellow students and co-workers to share the hope of the gospel. You grow in personal faith. You love and encourage the ordained workers and pastors; you worship Christ and give his church its concrete public expression in the world.

Of course you also grow tired. You sometimes slow down, or panic, or even wear out. You may even get on someone else's nerves.

Even so, in spite of all of the problems, the laity just as much as the pastors and workers are the church of Jesus Christ. They are the ones who volunteer their time and gifts to the ministry of Christ in the world. Most of those who make up the Christian advance team in the world are lay volunteers, the people of God in ministry.

Tom Gillespie, president of Princeton Theological Seminary, said at a meeting I attended recently: "Every institution has a spirit about it." The question is: Where do we find that "spirit" of a fellowship group or church? The spirit of a church I believe is more accurately seen among its volunteers than in the pages of its fund-drive full-color brochure. In fact, what happens in the lives of the lay Christian member of a fellowship is a more accurate measure of the character of a congregation or fellowship group than any other combination of spiritual life indicators. It is the bottom line.

Take a work crew at a Young Life camp. They work together through the several weeks of the summer. The campers come and are involved in a one-week heavy program designed for them. Nonetheless, what happens to the work crew may be of more crucial, long-term significance for the total strategy of the kingdom of God than what happens with the campers. Why? Simple: the campers, like churchgoers, may experience the "spirit of the institution," but the work crew are the labor force who by their discipleship shape that spirit.

If this is true, then we who mobilize lay volunteers need to think carefully about how to encourage these strategic folks so that they don't burn out. In this regard, I believe that four principles apply equally to the professional Christian servant and the lay volunteer.

Realistic Expectations
In the book of Acts, the church is first described as those repentant believers who received God's forgiveness in Jesus Christ and then were united in the "apostles' teaching and fellowship" (Acts 2:38-42). Note that this definition does not exclude or excuse any members of the church from these three criteria. We are all *inadequate* individuals who repent and receive grace. We are all being *taught* so that we may grow in the content of the gospel. And we all need *fellowship* with one another.

The essential truth here is that we are either volunteers or special "apostles" ("ones sent out") not because of our adequacy on a leadership flowchart, but because of grace. This is not to downgrade the need to develop our talents, but talents notwithstanding, we have all become Christians by grace. Thus, the most that anyone can expect from those of us in church work is *trust* in Christ, *growth* and *fellowship*. Each of these is a dynamic word that marks Christians as pilgrims.

Many of us, lay people as well as pastors, suffer because we create for ourselves greater expectations than this one given to us in Acts 2. We fashion an idealistic myth of what a leader is supposed to be. And while such myths are impressive and inspiring on paper, they are almost always false, since they are usually devoid of grace.

For that reason, we should test every occasion in our Christian community where volunteers are involved to see if these three criteria are being met.

Do the parents driving the kids to camp understand the spiritual objectives of the camp, so they can see the trip in the perspective of our goal to share the gospel with teen-agers?

Do they have a real chance for interaction and fellowship with each other and the kids?

Is there a teaching that happens to them so that they are not simply used as transporters?

I once spent a week at Laity Lodge in Texas, a Christian ministry sponsored by the H. E. Butt Foundation. On the first evening, the director Howard Hovde introduced each member of the lodge "family" to those of us who were guests for the week. Everyone was presented: the maids, student summer workers, dishwashers, volunteers from town, cooks. As he introduced each one, he told about their families, their local church involvement and their ministries. Then they themselves shared their concern for our week and their hopes that we, like they, would have a growing experience at Laity Lodge.

Consequently, that evening we all were bound together by a common gospel objective and a common fellowship. Burnout is much less frequent when those New Testament bonds are part of a paid employee's or volunteer's experience.

The Tyranny of Tiny Strings
Second, volunteers need the authority to move and flex and do

what needs to be done without what I call the tyranny of tiny strings. One of the worst kinds of oppression is the oppression of the faceless restraints of organizational timidity and distrust. Bureaucratic tyranny is a suffocating, antihuman feature in most authoritarian societies. It is the continuous, persistent and ever-present form of oppression in Soviet society, where every single move in a worker's life is fastened to small committees. The work-group leaders and Party committees, for example, must decide about housing requests, vacation requests and educational plans of every Soviet worker. It seems that each move is effectively slowed down by the bureaucratic wet cement of delayed decisions and endless procedures for approval.

In 1985 my family and I took a three-week train trip across the Soviet Union. It was our impression that Soviet citizens don't so much live under the fear of KGB tyranny as under the tyranny of a thousand tight strings which manage even the most ordinary day-to-day movement, restraining human flexibility, freedom and initiative.

Christian fellowships can also lose their ability to move decisively and flexibly because of the tight little strings of endless committee processes, needlessly deferred decisions and "management-by-objective" committees which freeze action in the here and now while we wait for long-range planning surveys to come in. In every living fellowship both large and small there must be a creative balance which enables people both to understand the larger policy goals and at the same time to act decisively and flexibly to meet situations without the hindrance of unnecessary institutional roadblocks.

Even some families, though they have no committees, are nevertheless bureaucratic in style because they never decide anything. This is why it is so refreshing to meet someone who is able to make a clean and definite decision without the need to check with others.

Of course, every fellowship needs checks and balances in policymaking, but the "spirit of the institution" should be one of good will, trust and adventure so that the experimenters and innovators are not squeezed out, but rather liberated to do concrete things under the guidance of the gospel.

This balance happens in direct proportion to the sense of shared consensus within the fellowship about what is major and what is minor. Such a consensus comes from healthy doctrine experienced in the community of faith by people who care · about each other because they have felt God's care. Christian care keeps us mellow enough to roll with the mistakes we inevitably make and yet able to act without unnecessary slowdown.

Beware of Power

The third principle is a necessary companion to the second. It's a warning: Beware of power! Both lay volunteers in Christian discipleship and Christian professional workers must guard against the temptation to abuse power—to tie strings on people and programs so that any movement requires our agreement.

When we give in to that temptation, we ourselves become the oppressors of initiative and creativity, and those who work with us must either obey us, humor us or deceive us in order to remain our coworkers. When we become preoccupied with power, our coworkers are eventually used up, one by one. Worse yet, they may resort to various survival games of deception in order to cope with a leader who has become intoxicated with power.

Notice the two nonproductive results. On the one hand, an abusive leadership style reaps a collection of noncreative, non-risk-taking leader-pleasers who impair a Christian fellowship's ability to meet challenges. On the other hand, abusive leaders find themselves surrounded by dishonest power brokers. Consequently, both professional worker and volunteer grow preoccupied with empire building and group politics.

How can we avoid succumbing to this temptation? We must begin with a healthy doctrine of power. In the New Testament authentic power is seen in Christ's concrete victory over sin, the devil and death; it is the life-giving and redeeming power of Jesus. For us as Christian leaders, therefore, authentic power is not the power we are able to exercise over other people but it is our confidence in the power of Christ. It is the authority that Christ himself has over all other powers. He is the one who by his death and resurrection has won the victory over the powers of sin and death and the evil one.

The greatest strength that we can ever know is our assurance of the permanent truth of this threefold victory and authority of Jesus Christ. We stand under his authority at all times and therefore whatever authority is entrusted to us is itself under the constant check and balances of the Law and the gospel.

Such a confidence is not oppressive toward others. On the contrary, it is freeing and contagious. The great continuity of the Christian church throughout history lies not in its institutional discipline or ordained pastoral authority, but rather in the gospel of the Living Word of God which the Holy Spirit confirms in people's lives down through the generations. It is the authority of truth and the life changed because of truth that has always been the real continuity of the church universal.

A Serious and Happy Task

The fourth and final principle applies to professionals as well as volunteers.

The key to a good ministry experience is recognizing that our work is both a serious task because of God's greatness and a happy task because of his companionship with us through his people. It can be an enjoyment as much as a task to drive teen-agers to a retreat, to wash dishes after the morning prayer breakfast, to tutor a youth who is struggling with math, to work in a community feeding program. The joy comes from knowing that we want to be where Christ is—serving his people, and serving strangers in his name. It is that joy of working with other Christians that keeps us refreshed.

Perhaps, after all, that's what the ancient psalmist meant when he said, "I would rather be a doorkeeper in the house of my God than dwell in the tents of wickedness" (Ps 84:10).

The Christian in the World

Chapter 7

The Mind Alive

I remember the senior class dinner at Princeton Seminary the year I graduated. The speaker was George Buttrick, who at that time was pastor at Madison Avenue Presbyterian Church in New York City. He challenged our class of future pastors in two directions.

First, he urged us to be with the people, to be listeners in the marketplace in order to understand where people are and what they are thinking and feeling. His second counsel seemed to contradict the first: "When you are at Coney Island, don't tell the people of the concessions on the boardwalk, about which they know; tell them of the mystery of the sea, about which they do not know." He went on: "Don't read only what your people are reading. . . . Read what your people are not reading."

Reading: The Key to a Mind Alive

He was impressing upon us the importance of having a mind that is alive. And that is good counsel for all Christians. As well as being physically well and spiritually committed, if we are to be effective Christians in the world we need to be intellectually growing and alert. We need to learn the mystery of the sea if we are to share that mystery with others or understand it ourselves.

There are various ways to keep our minds alive, but I think Buttrick was right to emphasize one—reading. I will do the same here.

In our world three questions quickly arise: First, how can I find time to read about the mystery of the sea when I have so many important responsibilities among the concessions? Second, when I have found the time, what should I read as a Christian in today's world? Third, if I do read, then how do I remember what I read?

In this chapter I will be mostly autobiographical, reflecting on some of my own experiences with these three problems. Although I write as a pastor, you will be able to adapt my experience to your situation. The principles illustrated are universal.

The Gift of Time

Each of us has been given the gift of time—twenty-four hours each day and the privilege of organizing it. None of us has more time than any other; the twenty-four hour rule is universal. Still, even in the face of pressures that differ from person to person, each of us has dominion over these twenty-four hours. Each of us is a steward of time.

This gift of time, of course, has its own snares, especially to those who are not self-starters, or who allow the hours of the week to confuse them into a random jumble of low-quality segments. This means that the first challenge which confronts the person who wants to study and read seriously is to have a clear philosophy of the week.

A Philosophy of the Week

For my own life as a pastor the key to having quality time for my family, for spiritual formation, for reading, for ministry to people, for writing and for recreation is to have a rhythm in each week. This means first of all that I think primarily in terms of seven-day periods rather than years, months or days. It is no mistake, it seems to me, that the seven-day week is the most basic biblical yardstick for life measurement. Six days thou shalt work and one day thou shalt rest: This means that a rhythmic week is commanded in the Fourth Commandment.

My goal, then, is to divide each week into a rhythm of work, rest, worship and play: of work with people—work alone; of worship with the community of faith—worship alone; of discussion—of reflection. A person is able to take in stride high intensity demands with their severe strains if there is also built into life the opportunity for an easing up of demand. It is also true that I am able to enjoy rest if time allotted to rest follows real work. I am talking about a rhythm that includes fast/slow, many/few, rich/lean, exterior/interior.

I divide my own week, for example, into two major parts: In the first part I place Sunday morning through Wednesday evening, which are for the large group meetings and worship services, also the counseling, small group study meetings and teaching sessions, and finally my church administration and staff obligations. Thursday and Friday are days for study, reflection, writing and reading. Friday evening through Saturday evening is family recreation time—a time for total change of pace.

My study goal each week is to have completed by Thursday noon the sermon for the coming Sunday. When this target is achieved, it then means that Thursday afternoon and Friday are available for long-term study for future sermons and also reading and writing. I find that if the immediate teaching, preaching preparation is not completed by Thursday, then that unfinished task tends to threaten and intimidate Friday and Saturday.

My week is intense at the beginning and eases up toward the end. Both halves of the week are of a better quality, it seems to me, when there is such a rhythm.

Choosing What to Read
Having scheduled the time and made it rhythmic, however we chose the segments, now the question is: What shall I read? I believe that the rhythm principle applies here too. I want to read intensively and also extensively; light and heavy; prose and poetry; theologically and geologically!

As a pastor my first intensive reading challenge is the main book of my life, the Bible. For me this means first of all having effective access to the original language texts and major translations of the Bible now available. It means a working library of historical background and technical books. Books by J. Jeremias and F. F. Bruce on the New Testament history; by Bruce Metzger on the New Testament text; theological dictionaries of the New Testament and Old Testament; the Brown, Driver, Briggs' Hebrew Lexicon, etc. I purchase exegetical and theological commentaries on a book-by-book basis.

In order to keep myself intellectually involved in theological dialog, I have pursued two reading goals. First, with regard to major theological writers, I have found that there are two ways into a heavyweight theological book: through the front door or by the window, that is, from the first page onward or through its topical, biblical reference index. Both are valid entrances into theological books. Often I find that the window route has coaxed me into reading the whole book.

A second way to keep engaged with current theological discussion is through journals and magazines. I read one set of journals faithfully: *Eternity, Christianity Today, Christian Century, Sojourners, Wittenburg Door, Radix, Theology Today, Youthworker Journal*. There is another set of scholarly journals that I try to catch up on each time I visit a seminary periodical room.

Most of the reading I have described to this point is wide and extensive, as in the case of journals, or it is research oriented, as in the case of theological books and commentaries. Another kind of reading has also been very important and rewarding for me. There are several authors with whom I have developed a special sort of friendship (they do not know me, but I know them). I am trying to read all that they have written. These are authors with whom I especially resonate, and it is my goal to have in my library a complete collection of their works.

My Friend the Author

These writers have become permanent friends. They are not masters of my mind, because I may not always agree with what they write; they are more like guides and companions who especially challenge me and who continue to encourage my own pilgrimage as a Christian. They are my mentors. I feel that I understand how they think and how they approach the serious questions. I not only read these writers, I reread them; and that is the real test of a book that is permanently important for a mind alive.

There are still other books and resources that I need because they open up some of the implications of faith that as a Christian and a pastor teacher I must pursue. I am thinking here of books on the world family, on economics, politics, psychology; books that demonstrate communication skills; books on the arts and music; books on Christian apologetics.

There are special interests that play a special role in each of our lives. Our reading should accompany us into these special interests. Since my University of California days as a political science student I have been vitally interested in political-social issues and my reading shows this interest. To this end I subscribe to *Foreign Affairs* and *The Christian Science Monitor*. I have had a special interest in historical and current affairs, communist world countries and World War 2 history.

O to Remember

Now comes the tough third question: How can I ever keep track of what I read and remember what needs to be remembered? For me the answer begins with the way I as a pastor see the study-reading task of my ministry. Is the pastor a collector, an assembler of the conclusions of others, or is the pastor a researcher-scholar who studies toward the goal of creative contribution?

The second model is the harder but by far the more rewarding. All of my reading is a vital part of the total research task that goes into and alongside the writing of a sermon or a special teaching study. My goal as a teacher/preacher is to do and present the results of original hard work on the text. Since this is so, then holding on to the discoveries that have resulted from reading is very important.

Slowly, Slowly

My own method is not complicated. I have found from experience that in order for me to remember what I have read, I must read carefully. Therefore, I read slowly. I take notes in the book itself or on a separate review page, or make coded marks in the margins of the book. I do not skim or speed-read the books that I feel are important. At the ends of chapters I ask myself to recount from memory the major arguments of the chapter. This technique helps me begin the process of in-depth comprehension of an author's thesis.

When I have found an unusually impressive book, I offer a small group seminar/discussion on it. This is another way to study a significant book creatively, as well as to see it through the eyes of other people.

Showing Respect

A book is a friend, and it is best remembered when we have a sense of respect for it. When I quote from authors in a sermon, my own approach is to quote few but long. I make use of only a few quotations in a given sermon, but they show respect for whatever is quoted. This means allowing the quotation to speak from its own setting; it means reading enough of the quotation so that the author is really heard and not simply used to focus on what I am saying.

This approach involves more work for the preacher homiletically in establishing the context for the quotation, but it also has the benefit of encouraging the listeners to read that author for themselves.

I have made for myself two rules for quotation. I do not quote from a book I have not read, and I do not quote from a typed card. I either quote from memory or read from the book itself, present and visible. In this way the book is honored, and also I believe endorsed to the listeners. It seems to me an insult to a great book like *Brothers Karamazov* to read selections from its great and moving chapters, now impertinently removed to utilitarian 3 x 5 cards. Such a great book deserves the fullest respect, not exploitation as literary embellishment.

Describing the Mystery of the Sea

As a pastor I stand in a long and good tradition of learning and of concern for truth. Books have their unique part to play in this lifelong obedience to truth, to which every Christian is committed. I am aware that electronic media, TV and films play an increasingly influential part in communication within the human family, but I still maintain that when it comes to the image building of that greatest of all collectors of dreams and ideas—the human mind—there is still nothing to match a book read aloud.

In *The Silver Chair* C. S. Lewis describes Jill's encounter with the lion Aslan: ". . . the voice was not like a man's. It was deeper, wilder, and stronger; a sort of heavy, golden voice. It did not make her any less frightened than she had been before, but it made her frightened in rather a different way." No TV set is able to capture or highlight the vast features of that golden lion quite so wonderfully as the human imagination itself set in motion by the words of a book.

The Book and books make it possible for us to describe the mystery of the sea.

My Special Friends

If I were to choose the most influential books in my own intellectual and spiritual pilgrimage, after the Bible, my list would look like this:

Blaise Pascal, *Pensees.* Here is the sheer excitement of a Christian mind alive to the relevance of Jesus Christ.

John Calvin, *Institutes.* His impressive grasp of the large outline of the gospel's meaning makes Calvin exciting.

Martin Luther, *Lectures on Romans.* As fresh and electric today as in the sixteenth century.

Karl Barth. Begin with *Dogmatics in Outline.* I deeply appreciate his boldness and his serious intention to hear and obey the biblical text. He is the theologian's theologian.

Dietrich Bonhoeffer. Begin with *Cost of Discipleship.* He called out to me to decide once and for all about what matters the most in my life.

C. S. Lewis. Begin with *The Chronicles of Narnia*. I owe so much to C. S. Lewis, especially the wonderful mixture of the surprise and goodness of God.

G. K. Chesterton. Begin with *The Everlasting Man* and *Orthodoxy*. I love his humor and ability to stir up my own imagination.

J. R. R. Tolkien, *The Lord of the Rings*. How can anyone miss out on the journey of Frodo and Sam Gamgee?

Helmut Thielicke. Begin with *How the World Began*. I learned about clearness in preaching from Thielicke.

Leo Tolstoy, Fyodor Dostoevski, Boris Pasternak, Alexander Solzhenitsyn. These Russian writers have stirred me emotionally and spiritually more than all other novelists.

T. S. Eliot, W. H. Auden, Robert Frost. These poets have given me a deep respect for words.

Mark Twain, Robert Benchley, for their rich humor and insight into personality.

Paul Tournier for his psychological wisdom and even-handedness. Try to find his book, *Secrets*.

I think the greatest novel I ever read is either *Crime and Punishment* or *The Brothers Karamazov*, both by Dostoevski; the greatest American novel is *Huckleberry Finn* by Twain. For me the most impressive recent novels are by Herman Wouk, *Winds of War* and *War and Remembrance*.

The most helpful book about the Christian faith for me has been Karl Barth's *Dogmatics in Outline*.

The most persuasive case for the Christian life, C. S. Lewis's *Screwtape Letters*.

For me the most impressive biographies have been *Karl Barth* by Eberhard Busch and *William Borden* by Mrs. Howard Taylor.

Chapter 8

The Meaning of Sex

"Only a clever human," wrote C. S. Lewis in *Screwtape Letters*, "can make a real joke about virtue, or indeed about anything else; any of them can be trained to talk as if virtue were funny. Among flippant people, the joke is always assumed to have been made. No one actually makes it; but every serious subject is discussed in a matter which implies that they have already found a ridiculous side to it. . . . It is a thousand miles away from joy; it deadens, instead of sharpening, the intellect; and it excites no affection between those who practice it."

Good Sex and Bad Jokes

I know what Lewis is talking about. I've seen the harm that

results from the flippancy he describes. Consider sex, for example. Most of us have told jokes in youth group meetings or among our friends that were perceived as both sexually aggressive and confusing by those who heard them.

But I'm ahead of myself. It is not my intention to scold you who are humorous and talented storytellers, but rather to look at what goes wrong in us to create the atmosphere of sexual aggression and confusion that is the deeper cause of bad jokes about sex and harmful attitudes that sometimes take over. (When I say *atmosphere,* I mean the way we look at ourselves and those who are around us.) Only when we understand our ills will we be able to build a healthy understanding of the mystery, the proper stewardship and the humor of sex. And this is just what we need to create a supportive atmosphere within the social groups that we are a part of and in our own private lives.

A Design and a Power

The word *sex* describes both a design and a power. The design is remarkable, first of all because it is so simple: "Male and female he [God] created them" (Gen 1:27). Yet in another sense, the design is not at all simple, because the interior and interpersonal realities of human sexuality are much like a musical score of the most intricate possibility and intensity. The design is a brilliant achievement in both senses—its simplicity and its colorful and humorous complexity.

Like every design, sexuality has its boundaries and its measurement scales which show how it takes its place in the larger whole of God's creative design. Yet we cannot understand the design, and especially the unique power, of sex without learning the meaning intended by the Grand Designer. Our relationships with our lovers, our families, the world around us and even ourselves all derive their deepest meanings from God's primary intentions in creation and redemption, in the way that he makes us and in the way that he forgives us when things go wrong.

The power of human sexuality is, first and foremost, the power of life itself. And if that were not enough, powerful feelings are at work as well in our decisions and our attitudes about sexuality. These feelings are such a dynamic part of our nature as male and female that it is impossible to discuss sexuality without thinking about the deeper implications of God's design.

What then is the grand intention of the Grand Designer for man and woman? I believe that part of the answer is found in the Bible's theology of dominion. Our sexual nature is a dominion given to us; God holds us accountable for that dominion.

For every dominion in life there is also a corresponding obligation; the dominion represented in our sexual nature has its positive affirmation of relationship between man and woman—marriage. This relationship is so important that the very expectation of its future prospect is the context for the ways that we relate to the opposite sex during the earliest years of our sexual awareness. This expectation shows itself in various ways, some serious and some playful; we are continually en route toward courtship and marriage as an expected goal even in our most youthful years.

The social fabric of every culture is profoundly involved in this pilgrimage from the separateness of childhood to the coupling of marriage. The story of this growing up is the story of greater and greater degrees of freedom and authority. For example, as knowledge increases, the human individual gathers more and more authority and power over the territories of ignorance and the unknown. What began as a small child counting five fingers on each hand gradually develops into geometry and calculus. With each increase in dominion there is a corresponding increase in responsibility for that part of our lives and nature over which we have power. This story is happening in every part of our personhood—physical dexterity, sexual development, intellectual capacity, spiritual growth.

The Restraint in Sexual Union

A Christian view of sexuality, based in both the Old and New Testaments, affirms that interpersonal restraint is the obligation properly assumed for the most intimate of all sexual experiences: sexual intercourse. Sexual union is understood in the Bible as a sign of that bonding of commitment between a man and a woman that we call marriage and family. The whole of each person is involved in the sexual intercourse of a man and woman. It is physical, emotional and spiritual communication, an event both playfully joyous and profoundly serious.

The restraint of sexual union between man and woman in the early years is a restraint that propels us toward the fulfillment of sexual union at the time of shared commitment. It is also a restraint of faithfulness by those who have made the commitment of marriage so that sexual union is reserved as the special language that only our partner in the bond of marriage is to know from us. By that gift to each other we share the oneness of marriage commitment.

The biblical words chosen to describe this encounter portray its mystery and its physical totality. The physical part is seen in the creation narratives: "Therefore a man leaves his father and mother and cleaves to his wife, and they become one flesh" (Gen 2:24). The emotional nature of sexuality is suggested by the verb *to know* as a term for intercourse: "Now Adam knew Eve his wife" (Gen 4:1). And the spiritual aspect is described by St. Paul: "This mystery is a profound one, and I am saying that it refers to Christ and the church" (Eph 5:32).

The Fear of Sex

Becoming aware of the all-encompassing importance of human

sexuality can be so overwhelming that we must be on guard against the one great danger that lies at the root of most of the harmful jokes and the deadness of flippancy that Lewis describes. That danger is fearing the awesomeness of sex so much that we become obsessively preoccupied with it.

The fear of sex is the real source of most of the bad jokes that appear so casual, just as fear is the source of most sexual confusion.

This may seem strange at first glance, but it is nevertheless true that fears about our sexual nature cause sexually chaotic behavior in some individuals and prudish interpersonal isolation and withdrawal in others. In both instances, the usual symptom is an unhealthy preoccupation with sex because of a profoundly deep fear of self and relationship which is the source of the symptom.

The Joy of Righteous Sex

In the biblical understanding of man and woman, however, there is no fear of the human body or its emotions, both of which are a vital part of our human design. Rather, it is because of the dignity of male and female sexuality that restraint and balanced stewardship are a part of biblical counsel. When we are able to grasp this biblical understanding and learn not to be afraid of sex, we are more able to enjoy its exciting meaning and even its sheer fun and silliness (the humorous perspective that is so essential to our spiritual and emotional balance), free from obsessive preoccupation.

How then does restraint—a concept that seems to carry with it only negative connotations—contribute to a joyful understanding of sex? Restraint, properly understood, works to our benefit because unlike restraint that is a punishment for something basically evil (such as being sent to your room without supper and TV because you were caught smoking cigarettes in the garage), Christian sexual restraint demonstrates a respect for something that is basically good and healthy.

I am reminded of a coach who places restraints on his players' activities to keep them healthy and properly conditioned for the coming game. A basketball player, for example, will be restrained by his coach from playing sandlot football during basketball season, not because his coach doesn't want him to have physical exercise, but because he wants to keep him healthy so that he can enjoy basketball to the fullest without a sandlot knee injury.

Alexander Solzhenitsyn has described this restraint with the term *self-limitation*. In his essay in behalf of world peace in *From Under the Rubble*, Solzhenitsyn argues that self-limitation and repentance are the proper responses of nations and people who recognize the crucial importance of seeing the great power for good or evil that is in the hands of people and nations as a part of the greater whole. Nuclear power therefore must be under restrained development in order to serve the world and not destroy the world.

Likewise, when we repent and ask forgiveness, we are admitting that a part of our lives has lost its way in confusion, and we now turn toward the Lord of new beginnings for help and restoration. Self-limitation admits that each of the powerful possibilities of my life need discipline in order to achieve their fulfillment.

Some Pleasant Surprises

There are some pleasant surprises for us here. One is that when we fail and when we make mistakes sexually, the God of . the grand design is also the healer of all confusion when we seek his help in earnest repentance. But most of all we make the discovery that God is more concerned about our happiness than we are. He is the one who designed us. He knows how we are put together. When we remember God's great design with its meaning and goal, then we are able to enjoy the humorous and unpredictable way that God has made us as men and women, and the way he has fine-tuned our feelings and desires. Then there is a rich humor in it all which should never be forgotten.

The adventures of growing up, of falling in love, of making lifelong commitments and all the unique possibilities of the way our personalities work are whimsically fun, just as they are seriously important. It is this basic humor in the way that God made us that is the source of the wonderfully funny stories about our sexuality and our romantic behavior. By all means, let's tell those stories to our heart's content.

The Four Uses of Money

What do we do about money? Almost everyone I know has trouble with it. In fact, we have problems two ways: Either it burns a hole in our pocket or it sticks to our fingers.

The Problem of Money
The problem is a very old one. Jesus himself talked so much about money that it is the most persistent single theme in his parables.

Jesus tells of laborers who work different lengths of time and yet receive the same money at the end of the day. He tells of a landowner who gives each of his stewards a mina (three-months' wages) and then holds them accountable for the ways in which they steward that trust. Jesus tells of a son who asked his father for his share of an inheritance so that he could leave home with the money in his hand. He tells of a Samaritan who paid an innkeeper two denarii (two days' wages) to care for a victim of highway violence. He tells of the person who bought a field because in that field was a pearl of great value. He even tells of a lost silver coin that a woman searches her house in order to find.

Money fascinates us as much as it bothers us, and therefore every story or parable that makes use of money as a part of the story will always catch our attention. Marriage counselors have discovered from their study of marriages in stress that decisions and worry about money are the most common cause of serious disagreement between married couples, a greater source of conflict than sex.

The Key Questions

The questions for Christians to face are these: What am I to do with money when I have it? And how do I keep my life in perspective when I have either too little or too much?

Money is a good thing, and it should be spent. The issue of how to use money is fundamentally a question of balance and skill. It sounds simple enough. But how do we develop the skill to keep our balance?

Money Is Property

First we need to know what money is. Money is both property (in a fixed territorial sense) and the dynamic opportunity for dominion (that is, a freedom possibility). It comes either as a gift we receive or it is earned by hard work.

Money is an asset, and it is a power. As an asset, it is a part of our concreteness; as a power, it is a part of our freedom.

What I mean is that the concreteness of property is a part of our earthly identity, our continuity with the created world. Your clothing is an extension of your personhood just as is your skateboard, your camera, your house. For example, your tape cassette collection gives an unmistakable imprint of your personhood, your values, your dreams.

It is because of this connection that the Tenth Commandment warns each of us against the lustful coveting of the property of others. Property is part of the extension of our life space. This is the reason that land reform is so vital in developing, rural countries today. Ordinary people need to feel a sense of real ownership of the land that they till and the houses they live in. Cities become livable too when people feel a concrete connection to the streets and houses where they live. Property ownership becomes meaningful and a valid expression of human dignity.

Money Is Power

There is also a power in money: money is the indicator of authority opening the way for various possibilities of action. We use money to do things we want to do. As such it expresses our freedom and therefore our stewardship responsibility.

The concreteness and the freedom that money symbolizes are indeed interconnected and are both pointers that set apart human beings as the only creatures in the order of creation that use money or understand its symbolic significance.

Money and Idolatry

Before we can answer the question "How do I use money?" we must face another question: "How do I keep from belonging to money?" The problem here is idolatry, and there are two kinds we need to confront: the idolatry of concreteness and the idolatry of dominion. Both are attempts on our part to find and project meanings upon some one part of the created order that it does not legitimately have in and of itself.

When we reach out to a thing and ask or insist that it grant basic meaning to our lives, we have created an idol. We have engraved either our desires or our fears upon some part of the whole of creation and we have treated that part as if it were the source of the whole or as if it were more essential than it is.

Idolatry sometimes happens to us without our own awareness that it is happening. It is not that we consciously worship possessions but in fact they have used up our ability to concentrate on anything else. We collect too many things for our own good. We end up unbalanced by the awkward sizes and shapes of the things we own. It becomes hard to move and act decisively because fixed assets have used up the space we need to think clearly about what we care most about. We are too "heavy" to travel; what we own is so costly, we cannot risk leaving anything behind.

Things are like plants that need water; they finally demand so much water that the riverbanks of our lives give way. What was meant to be a steady stream going somewhere focused and definite becomes a swamp of random, aimless pools. Even our interpersonal relationships are exploited and harmed by the confusion of the ownership of possessions and the things that go with them.

Remember Father Tim in *Mass Appeal?* The interchange between him and Mark shows the entrapping power of things:

Mark: All right. I don't understand.

Tim: This is my home. The people know me. They know my favorite colors—the kind of sweaters I like—my favorite wine. Do you know what a town in Iowa is like? There might be a Main street. If there is a movie theatre, it only shows family movies. The people would not understand my humor. They wouldn't talk to me. I have to talk to people.

Tim cannot move decisively because he has lost his freedom to move. A Mercedes and his favorite colors are not the whole story, but they are part of it.

Along with an attachment to things, there can also be a captivity to the dynamic nature of money. This produces a person who is permanently on the move—something like an overscheduled tourist. We use money in this case to buy distance and a certain kind of freedom. Money equals speed and maneuverability, and in this dynamic form it is the maneuverability itself that becomes a tempting demon of power.

Each kind of captivity—collecting and doing—is damaging to balance and to priorities. One is like glue on our fingers when we are trying to sort pictures: the other is like a paint that won't stick to anything. The Collectors can only tell about what they own or are now buying; the Doers can tell where they plan to go next week.

Four Uses of Money

As I see it, there are only four uses for money: We can use money to do good; we can save and invest it for our own future good and the good of others; we can pay bills; and we can use it for adventures. Each of these four uses can be relatively free (never totally, because we grow in grace with ups and downs) from the destructive distortions of idolatry as long as we commit this concrete and dynamic nature of our existence to the lordship of Jesus Christ.

When we really trust in the will of God for us in regard to our money, we can begin to experience the power of Christ's love to fulfill our lives. Such fulfillment sets us free from the captivity of money much more thoroughly than any warning against selfishness could ever do.

Recently I taught a course at New College Berkeley on the Ten Commandments. One of my students, Quentin Kuhran, a young businessman, wrote a paper discussing the commandment "Thou shalt not steal." He wrote:

"Ultimately to desire, and to try to obtain, the property of another is to be dissatisfied with what God has given, and thus to show lack of faith in His love" (Quoted from R. Alan Cole's *Exodus* commentary).

These interpretations are very insightful and we would do well to aggressively follow them with the wholeness of our heart. But is there something else that can be construed from this powerful commandment?

I believe this commandment calls us to go beyond restraining either an emotion to desire, or seizure of another's property. I believe we are called to give to our neighbor.

Even though the formal language is negative, the implications are grandly positive. Consider the following contrasts:

"You shall have no other gods before Me"—negative

"You shall love the Lord your God"—grand positive

"You shall not take the name of the Lord your God in vain"—negative

"You shall take the name of the Lord thy God in earnest"—grand positive

The grand positive of this commandment is, I believe, twofold:

(1) You shall love your neighbor as yourself, and

(2) You shall give to your neighbor.

Kuhran is describing the freedom from money that enables a man or woman to really have maneuverability in a positive way set free from the destructive and spoiling power of idolatry. Then it is that we are able to do good with both the concrete assets and the power that they represent.

What we do with money we are doing with the earth as stewards of the earth. So it is not surprising that the four uses of money take a large part of each day in every person's life. Each of the four uses has its positive and its negative possibility.

Doing Good

First, just as we are to do good with the earth, we are to do good with our money. *Edify* is the biblical word meaning "to do good," "to build up." And we know from the New Testament that everything we make and do is tested by that standard. Did we do good with what we had of time and talent and the resources of the earth? Did our use of these resources encourage others? This is the test.

The Old Testament principle of tithing is a sign of recognition that all of the bounty of the earth is to be under our stewardship. That is, we are to use this bounty according to God's revealed will. Tithing, giving a tenth of our resources to help those outside of our own families, is a practical way of expressing our agreement with this first goal in the use of all property and power that has found its way into our hands.

For Future Good

Money may also be saved for future good, just as part of every harvest must be set aside for future planting. This stewardship mandate warns us against the careless exploitation of present resources without concern for the generation that follows our own.

When we go to school and learn a skill, we are deeply involved in doing good by investing in the future. Right now students are at work in labs and classrooms; some, for example, are learning the stewardship skills to help the inhabitants of our planet solve the problems of the erosion of the ozone layer that lies as a thin protective shield around our globe. Every dollar, yen or pound that is invested in their education fulfills the first two purposes of the use of money.

Likewise, as we invest our money and time in the lives of people so that they discover God's love and forgiveness, we have answered the call to spend our money well.

Our Daily Bread

The third use of money is immediate and often urgent. We use money to eat and keep warm and so that our family may eat too. This third use of money is not taken lightly in the Bible. Our Lord placed the urgent daily need for bread into the heart of the prayer he taught to his disciples: "Give us this day our daily bread."

It is an interesting psychological and sociological fact that those who have never been poor cannot imagine how poor people can use money in any other than this way. They assume that only the rich have other options. In their mind philanthropy is synonymous with wealth. "He was a rich philanthropist," we say. The opposite is more likely to be true: The poor are more generous than the rich.

Poor people save their money for the education of children; poor people have done good with their money. And like the widow in the gospel account, they often give generously to the needs of others. Moreover the poor celebrate: They have barrio fiestas and build cathedrals too!

It is the usually wealthy who tell the false story that the poor care only about bread on the table. It is the wealthy radical, not the poor, who is most cynical about money spent on music and cathedrals.

The Adventure

Finally there is the adventure. An adventure is a very good way to spend money and can have permanent good results. An adventure is a shared experience that you can talk about for the rest of your life. It usually costs a lot less than a car, but unlike a car, it appreciates in value.

For one person an adventure may be a concert, for another a white-river rafting expedition. For one it may be travel, for another a stamp collection. For one it is building a church building, for another a barrio fiesta. In each instance money enables things to come into our hands for us to use, or for chances to go places and exercise dominion creatively and positively.

My advice is that we aim to include an adventure in our lives as soon as possible. It is one of the best ways to outwit the "need" to buy a new car or color TV. It also proves that our solemn responsibility to be stewards is not just good but fun. You see, most adventures are more experiences than possessions. Though, of course, some equipment may be necessary, the equipment is not the primary goal but only the means.

It is not biblically sound to understand stewardship in such serious terms that the joy of adventure is lost as a valid stewardship ingredient. It is St. Paul who reminded the Philippians that he knew how to be "abased" and also how to "abound."

As a family, my wife Shirley and our three children (Anne, Jon and Elizabeth) have aimed for adventure experiences, and they have given us a wonderful bonding event to add to all other joy and sorrow bonding. Just as work bonds a family, so does play.

The truth of the matter is this: I will enjoy the use of money when I am free from the domination of money over my life. This is a practical result of such systematic stewardship goals as tithing. I recognize the responsibility of giving right off the top of my earnings and resources. I have already agreed that what is in my bank account just as what is in my skilled hands belongs to the Lord. It is the idolaters who cannot enjoy possessions because to them possessions have taken on too much symbolic significance. It is the man or woman who sees all of life in the context of Christ's reign who can really abound. They can use money to enable an adventure.

I believe all four uses of money are valid in their time and season. It is hard work that creates money, either the work we have done or the work of someone else. But in each instance the result is money which is ours to use in all four ways.

Most cathedrals and churches have been built as the adventures of ordinary folk, just as the support of the mission and ministry of the church worldwide is not the result of foundation grants, but of millions of ordinary people who enjoy giving.

There are four things to do with money, and the key to the art of staying healthy is that we do all four. By all means money should be spent, and these are the ways to enjoy doing just that.

Chapter 10

The Journey of Reconciliation

Peace **is a great** word. It even sounds good when we hear it spoken: whether in Hebrew, *shalom*, in Arabic, *saliim*, or in English, *peace*. It is what the world we live in today needs but neither knows how to have nor how to keep.

The Meaning of Peace

Peace has profound ethical meanings for the Christian and is a key word in Jesus' most famous sermon. Jesus opened the Sermon on the Mount with nine blessings. One goes as follows: "Blessed are the peacemakers, for they shall be called sons of God" (Mt 5:9). What does it mean to be a peacemaker? What is peace anyway.

Peace is an important word throughout the Bible. We first see it as the Hebrew word *shalom*, used some 250 times in the Old Testament. About 25 times *shalom* is used as a greeting or farewell. Some 50-60 times it carries the meaning of reconciliation or peace, safety after strife, as for example in 1 Kings 4:25. But in the majority of uses (two-thirds of all instances) *shalom* means *fulfillment, wholeness, health,* as in Isaiah 54:10.

New Testament students know that the Old Testament words have the most significant affect upon New Testament words and meanings, so that even though it is written in first-century Greek, the thinking and approach to life that undergirds New Testament language is more Hebrew than Greek. This is clearly the case with the word *peace.* It is the rich content of *shalom* that *decisively* influences the appearance and use of the words for peace in the New Testament.

Three Greek Words

One way to test this influence is to note the way that *shalom* is translated into Greek in the Septuagint, the Greek translation of the Old Testament, which according to Jewish tradition was written about 100 B.C. by seventy Hebrew rabbis. Because even by that time Jewish people involved in trade and commerce were already scattering throughout the Mediterranean world, it was necessary for the Jewish community to have a text of the Old Testament written in Greek, that is, in the common language of the first-century world. In that translation the rabbis used three Greek words to translate the 250 usages of *shalom* in the Old Testament.

One word used was *telos,* which means *fulfillment* and carries the sense of wholeness.

Another word they used was *sozo* which is the root word for *to save.* Thus all of the salvation vocabulary of the New Testament has a relationship to the shalom vocabulary of the Old Testament.

The third word is *eirene* which carries within it in classical Greek usage the sense of "absence of strife" and therefore harmony.

The surest way to understand what this word means is to watch it closely as it is used in each particular text of Old Testament or New Testament sentences. When we do that, we discover three meanings for the words for peace in the Bible.

Three Dimensions of Peace

First, *peace* is presented in Old and New Testament texts as a word that derives its force and meaning from a greater source. Like the language of *faith, hope, and love, peace* is a word that gains its full meaning from its source. Peace is a gift that has its origin in God's decision and action. Peace comes from God as in Psalm 29:11:

May the LORD give strength to his people!

May the LORD bless his people with peace!

Second, *peace* is used to describe the *result* of God's act in the lives of human beings. It is in this sense that peace and righteousness (justice) cannot be separated. In other words, *peace* means more to the writers of the Bible than mere absence of conflict. We must, in fact, use words like *fulfillment* and *health* to really catch its complete meaning in the Bible.

Paul has this in mind when he encourages the Corinthians to "live in peace." "Finally, brethren, farewell. Mend your ways, heed my appeal, agree with one another, live in peace, and the God of love and peace will be with you" (2 Cor 13:11).

The third meaning of *peace* in the Bible is the active sense of peace as an experience and process of reconciliation that takes place in the midst of the pressures of personal and external turbulence. Our Lord assures his disciples that "in the world you have tribulation." Nevertheless, there is a peace that he will grant to them in the midst of that turbulence. This is the powerful peace that Jesus is describing in John 16:33: "I have said this to you, that in me you may have peace. In the world you have tribulation; but be of good cheer, I have overcome the world." Here is the peace that reconciles and draws into relationship those who are alienated. The apostle Paul puts it dramatically when he says:

Therefore, since we are justified by faith, we have peace with God through our Lord Jesus Christ. (Rom 5:1)

For if while we were enemies we were reconciled to God by the death of his Son, much more, now that we are reconciled, shall we be saved by his life. (Rom 5:10)

Two Levels of Reconciliation

I want to, in more detail, reflect upon this third understanding of peace in the Bible—the task and experience of peace as reconciliation. The word *reconcile* in Greek is the root of the English word *catalyst,* and it means an intervention in favor of conflicting parties who are caught up in a warfare so that a new resolution is the result.

Reconciliation is a journey that moves through two levels on its way from alienation toward wholeness, from division to the place of agreement. Let us examine those two parts of reconciliation so that we may be equipped to be peacemakers in a world deeply alienated spiritually, interpersonally and internationally.

The First Stage: Restraint/Repentance

The first stage in the journey of reconciliation is the experience of restraint/repentance. Here is the slowing down and clearing away of debris so that the next and deeper level of reconciliation may be experienced. When this first stage of the journey happens to us and upon us by outward action, we call it "restraint." When it happens from within us, we call it "repentance."

Restraint is not peace, but it is an important part of the journey toward peace. It is what happens when a boundary appears across the pathway of our lives so that we are compelled to slow down. John records a decisive example of restraint in his gospel. They went each to his own house, but Jesus went to the Mount of Olives. Early in the morning he came again to the temple; all the people came to him, and he sat down and taught them. The scribes and the Pharisees brought a woman who had been caught in adultery, and placing her in the midst they said to him, "Teacher, this woman has been caught in the act of adultery. Now in the law Moses commanded us to stone such. What do you say about her?" This they said to test him, that they might have some charge to bring against him. Jesus bent down and wrote with his finger on the ground. And as they continued to ask him, he stood up and said to them, "Let him who is without sin among you be the first to throw a stone at her." And once more he bent down and wrote with his finger on the ground. But when they heard it, they went away, one by one, beginning with the eldest, and Jesus was left alone with the woman standing before him. Jesus looked up and said to her, "Woman, where are they? Has no one condemned you?" She said, "No one, Lord." And Jesus said, "Neither do I condemn you; go, and do not sin again." (Jn 8:1-11)

A woman is caught in the act of adultery and brought by a crowd to Jesus as he taught in Jerusalem. The crowd is apparently prepared to stone her and follow the letter of the Law in Leviticus even though such a mob action would be in violation of Roman law.

If a man commits adultery with the wife of his neighbor, both the adulterer and the adulteress shall be put to death. (Lev 20:10)

They ask Jesus for his judgment, "What do you say about her?" According to the gospel-writer John, the crowd is posing the question cynically and for ulterior motives. They ask him his opinion in order to tempt him. But Jesus does not answer their question. Instead, he does two things: He bends down to write in the sand; and as they continue to put pressure on him to speak, he turns the question toward each of them, "Who of you are sinless. . . ?"

Both by what he does and says, Jesus restrains the crowd. First, he bends over and writes on the ground, thus slowing everything down and creating a nerve-racking, kingly silence. This is restraint. His words to the crowd become a boundary for those who thought they were ready to stone their prisoner to death. "From the eldest to the youngest they went away." This is restraint. It is not resolution; it is not salvation, but it is the essential first step before a resolution can happen. It is a boundary that protects the people from doing more harm than has already been done.

Time Out!

Jesus placed himself as a barrier across the pathway of cumulating violence. This sort of restraint happens in our century when alarmed neighbors rush into the hallway of a dorm to stop a fight between two students. It is the role a peace officer plays in attempting to stop a crime in progress. It is the role of the multinational, peacekeeping, military presence in a country like Lebanon. Such restraint is not a lasting solution to the complicated mixture of ancient and recent suspicion, injustice and fear that is present in the various population groups and nations of the Middle East or any other social situation, but the restraint of a cease-fire or a truce is, nevertheless, a necessary part of the whole journey.

Restraint, therefore, is intervention from forces outside of our lives so that a slowing down happens. This slowing down should never be confused with the peace that is the wholeness of health and resolution, but it is certainly better than the violence that only compounds the damage already done.

Put Down That Rock!

The ways that restraint takes place are sometimes incongruous and even humorous. I remember a riot in Berkeley during the spring of 1972. A car had been overturned by the rioters just in front of our church at the corner of Dana Street and Channing Way. As two Berkeley firemen were attempting to spray foam over the spilling gasoline, a crowd began to jeer them and several people were throwing rocks at them.

I was upset by the whole event when in front of me a young man took up a rock to throw. Suddenly, and with my most authoritative voice, I said to him, "What are you doing with that rock? I'm pastor of this church, and that rock is church property. You're not going to throw that rock because it belongs to First Presbyterian Church. So, put it down."

The young man looked at me and laughed and threw the rock down. He walked away and said cheerfully to me, "I used to be a pacifist too." Actually I wasn't so much a classical philosophic pacifist as a simple restrainer, at least in this case. He had been temporarily protected by my command from the cowardly act he was about to commit with one of our rocks. There was no time to grapple with the deeper intellectual, political, religious issues and feelings of rage or fear or even boredom that brought him to where he was on that afternoon; but at least one barrier had forced him to slow down and hesitate. Besides, at least my command had protected a fireman trying to prevent the disaster of a gasoline fire in which everyone would have been the loser.

Repentance—Inner Restraint

The restraint that happens from within us is what the Bible calls repentance. Repentance has several ingredients, one of the most important being self-restraint. Here we ourselves realize the harm that is happening to us and through us so that we ourselves decide to stop and look for a step toward peace. The prodigal son "comes to himself," and decides to find his way back to his father (Lk 15:11-32). Peace does not automatically come by his decision to repent—to admit his moral and spiritual guilt—but he does begin to head in the right direction. He turns toward the relationship where to his surprise he unexpectedly finds resolution and healing and peace through the amazing grace of his waiting Father.

Our world badly needs to take this early step on the journey of reconciliation. It's the first step toward a more substantial total resolution. Alexander Solzhenitzyn in *From Under the Rubble* has called upon the great nations of the world to embrace this value. He calls it the "old Christian" value of self-restraint. His argument is powerful and timely:

> After repentance, comes self-limitation. Repentance creates the atmosphere for self-limitation. Self-limitation on the part of individuals has often been observed and described, and it is well-known to all of us; but as far as I know, no state has ever carried through a deliberate policy of self-limitation or set itself such a task in general form. Though when it has done so at difficult moments in some particular sector, such as food rationing or fuel rationing, then self-limitation has paid off handsomely.

Restraints, both from within or without, are not in themselves peace; but they do offer us time and opportunity. A truce is not a treaty, but it does offer breathing and thinking and negotiating space.

This time to think and repent is precisely what Jesus provides to the crowd in Jerusalem and also to the accused woman with whom he speaks. "Where are your accusors?" he asks.

"They have all left, Lord."

"Neither do I accuse you. Go and sin no more."

Jesus has interposed his own person and authority into an angry and volatile incident, and to both the mob and the lonely, accused woman he has given the gift of time—time to think, to wonder, to repent, to decide. In John's account, the very next words of Jesus are these: "Again Jesus spoke to them, saying, 'I am the light of the world; he who follows me will not walk in darkness, but will have the light of life' (Jn 8:12). Restraint is intended in God's design to be one part of the longer journey that leads to righteousness.

Making Peace

We who live under God's grace are grateful for restraint; we see it as one more sign of God's grace. We do not glorify this time and opportunity, but we are grateful for it. In fact, we should work hard for it in the world situation of our generation so that the greater goals of *shalom* may be realized. There needs to be the restraint of civilization and of the organization of societies in the social contract so that human beings can be as close to each other as possible without doing harm to each other.

As Christians we eagerly work for the fullest possibilities of relationship with people because we have the good news of God's peace to share with our neighbors. Since God's peace is able to heal human brokenness, the people of that peace have all the more reason to work hard for the temporary cease-fires and truces that allow for time and relationship building. This is a strong argument in favor of Christians who plan careers in such professions as law enforcement and politics.

As I see it, one of the major moral flaws in blood revolution or the bloody suppression of the threats of insurgency is that after such runaway vengeance, when finally all is quiet on the western front, we discover in grief that people have died who might have been reconciled. But now there is no longer opportunity for that.

The Final Stage: the Peace of Righteousness

But what is peace at the deeper level? Let us return to first principles. The Lord who gave to us the peacemaking mandate has also given to us the whole peace to go with it. It is a fourfold peace that restores relationship toward *God, myself, my neighbor* and *the earth.* It is the peace that has righteousness as its result. It is the peace that takes time to build because it is dynamic and not static. It is the peace we submit to in faith as we trust in Jesus Christ to be our savior and to grant his peace to us. It is the ministry of peacemaking that happens as ordinary Christians with the equipment of the gospel stay close to where people really live and study and work. If you are planning your future career, why not give yourself to a peacemaking career at some place along the vital continuum we have been discovering?

One of my favorite scenes in the children's stories of C. S. Lewis, The Chronicles of Narnia, takes place in *The Lion, the Witch and the Wardrobe* following immediately after Aslan's great victory over the witch at the stone table. Lucy and Susan are invited to join Aslan and run throughout the land setting free those who have been turned to stone during the oppressive reign of Jadis, the winter witch. Before they ride on Aslan's back, the Great Lion himself had to become their peace and heal the treachery of Edmund their brother. But Aslan not only resolved the treachery of sin, he also healed the fears of each of the sons and the daughters of Adam.

We cannot do the work of peacemaking until there is peace in our own lives. Just as in the divine logic of biblical ethics, we are not commanded to share love until we first experience love. "Beloved, let us love one another" (1 Jn 4:7). So it is with peace: "I have said this to you, that in me you may have peace. In the world you have tribulation; but be of good cheer, I have overcome the world" (Jn 16:33).

Section III

Sheer Encouragement

C h a p t e r   1 1

Sheer Encouragement

Has it dawned on you that you belong to a family that is like no other in the world? There are secrets that you know and ways you do things that make you different.

Sometimes it is embarassing when your family connection is exposed. Maybe when you were a teen-ager your mother or father kissed you in front of your friends just as you were getting out of the car at summer camp. But sometimes it is profoundly and powerfully wonderful as your pride is stirred because a friends at school tell you how great they think your mom is.

Sheer encouragement is a good gift to give to anyone, and the people from whom we first receive this gift (if we are fortunate) are our parents. This gift is one of the best parents have in their power to bestow. It always does good. It can be had in great supply, no matter the economic welfare of the family, for it can be drawn from the resources of God himself.

In the Bible, it is the gift most often noted in the advice given to parents. It is even a vow parents make at the baptism of an infant; they agree to raise their children "in the nurture and the encouragement of the Lord."

Sheer Encouragement
But what is *sheer encouragement?* What are its mysterious secrets? How do we learn them? And how do we give sheer encouragement to our own children and to others around us? How do we compensate when sheer encouragement has not been our experience either from parents or mentors or friends? In order to answer these questions we must understand what encouragement is and what it is not.

Sheer encouragement can be characterized in at least four ways. First, since it begins with the encourager, encouragers must themselves be encouraged. Next, it involves respect and discipline. And finally it is fun.

Encouraging the Encourager
First, encouragement begins inside my own heart and mind. This means that in order to share its good effects with those around me, I need to discover God's love and faithfulness myself.

Encouragement needs daily renewal because last week's encouraging phone call may not be adequate to help us withstand the pressures of today's trials. The continuous nature of the gift means that we who want to encourage others must have renewable sources of encouragement for our own lives. That source must be a conviction of our own worth, so that we feel encouraged by God to be who we are and where we are.

Only then can we encourage our children and our friends

without the subtle "hooks" that spoil so much of what some-times passes for "encouragement." There are parents, for ex-ample, who cheer their children toward achievements in aca-demic work, sports, the arts, or even the church—not out of the fullness of grace, but out of half-filled and frustrated parental ambitions, now programmed into the lives of their children. Such encouragement is anything but sheer. In fact, it is just the opposite—a highly controlled endorsement strategy that orig-inates in hidden agendas, now being fulfilled through the ex-periences of sons and daughters so that we become "encourag-ers" who are pushing another person to succeed in order to complete our own incompleteness.

I know of only one safeguard against this kind of fraudulent encouragement, and that is the spiritual and emotional health of the encourager. This is why we must begin our reflections on the gift of encouragement with a close look at ourselves.

The Lord of Encouragement
Where do we find the kind of encouragement that can be given away with no strings attached? We will always find that the good verbs of life, like *love* and *encourage*, have their source sooner or later in the great Noun, the Lord of love who is the Lord of encouragement.

This means that to keep encouragement free from the con-tamination of my selfish and sometimes hidden motivations I must feel the sheer safety and goodness of God's love for me. When I am assured of this profound inner encouragement, then I am able to really encourage others. It is the apostle Paul who sensed the fullness of God's love for his own life and who was therefore able to encourage his friends at Philippi: "And my God will supply every need of yours according to his riches in glory in Christ Jesus" (Phil 4:19). There are no hooks in that sentence.

"I Don't Get No Respect"

"Mother always held my older brother's hand when they crossed the street. Me she sent alone," laments Rodney Dangerfield. "I just don't get no respect."

The second characteristic of sheer encouragement is respect. Respect for our children and the people in our lives acts as a strong limitation on the "hooks" and hidden agendas of fraudulent encouragement. Unlike Rodney Dangerfield, I was always taken seriously by my mother and father, and that one single aspect of their encouragement kept typical paternalism and maternalism under manageable control during the years of my growing up.

We always talked a lot, disagreed, agreed to disagree and found agreement too. At the center of the talking in our home as I was growing up was my mother and father's basic respect for us children and for our ideas too, and this regardless of our age. Though children are advised in the Bible to honor and respect their parents, respect is a two-way street. Mutual respect in a home produces not only a truly educated child, but also an encouraged one. In fact, there are few experiences in life as robust and encouraging as the spirited conversations of people who are genuinely listening to each other because they respect each other.

Our Children Are Not Our Own

At an infant's baptism, the parents receive the child back into their hands from the pastor, who announces the child's Christian name for the whole congregation to hear. In that announcement, we parents agree that our children are not our property or the extension of our own bodies; they are unique individuals of dignity and worth because of God's promise and decision. Therefore, we must raise them up as the most important guests in our homes. They don't actually belong to us; they are entrusted to us. Respecting the individual's worth in this way enables family members to face one another realistically without excuses.

Because the grace of forgiveness underpins all proper respect, we experience the realism that goes with the encouragement that has its origin in the gospel of Jesus Christ. We are respected for what we are. Despite our shortcomings, those who respect us listen closely to what we say; they try to hear us. Thus there is an earnestness in relationships that sets us free to think things through for ourselves; we come to feel that our thoughts matter. We sense this respectfulness in the encounters of Jesus with people throughout the Gospel narratives. Everyone Jesus meets has his full attention.

Disciplined Pressure toward Growth

The third characteristic of encouragement is discipline. Discipline coaches us toward knowledge and skill in hands and mind; discipline trains us in character and self-control. It helps a growing person reach his or her best stride (and this goal of edification is the test by which all methods of discipline should be judged).

No real encouragement is possible apart from such a healthy pressure toward growth. We need those teachers and parents who make demands of us for our own good. The result is that we are encouraged to grow. At the same time the balanced influence of these demands give us a "reality check" on our developing self-awareness.

The Stress that Destroys

Discipline is healthy pressure, healthy stress. This is in total contrast to bad pressure which is what the Bible calls temptation.

Temptation presses us toward bad choices and away from

hope. Discipline encourages us to decide and act toward truth and knowledge. The goal of discipline is to strengthen; the goal of temptation is to destroy. In discipline stress is necessary; without stress on the heart muscle it cannot be thickened and made more efficient in its recovery rate after strong exertion. But in temptation the stress on our lives seeks to destroy and is therefore always evil. Discipline is good and profoundly encouraging because it signals how seriously my life and growth is being taken by someone else. They not only know that I exist, but they want me to succeed.

But since discipline involves the handling of another person's life, it takes skill, time and work for the teacher and also time for the learner. There is no easy way to learn math or French or anything else that is important. Consequently, encouragement cannot afford to be indulgent or sloppy. It is concerned to prepare the person for the road, not the road for the person.

The Shared Fun Instinct

Finally, sheer encouragement is characterized by what I call the shared fun instinct. The kind of encouragement usually cherished longest in our memory is the inadvertent, unplanned event (often on the way home from a seemingly more important event) when the family or a group of friends simply has fun together and enjoys the simple fact of one another's existence. It happens when you discover that you not only love your children and your parents but you genuinely like them too— they're fun to be around.

If I want to encourage someone, I will let them know every day in a different, unplanned way that they please me and that I am simply proud to be their father, or their youth leader, or their friend, or their son.

Fun is a powerful force for encouragement. This is why

heartfelt laughter is so healing. The thin laughter of cynicism has an opposite effect. Because it is sustained at someone else's expense, it builds up an inevitable debt of anger and bitterness. But there is sheer encouragement in sheer laughter, and its result is as ethically good as it is physically healthy. Families need fun events where children and parents laugh together, just as they need heavy moments together where parents and children cry together. Only human beings laugh and cry, and we must have both to remind us of our humanness.

The Legacy of Grief
The legacy of genuine joy is encouraging but so is the legacy of genuine grief. Our experiences of sorrow become a grand and wondrous part of the encouragement mandate that parents have toward their sons and daughters, or close friends are able to share together. A stranger will not cry with you at some very small but real defeat that your heart feels, and this opaqueness of social and interpersonal distance is discouraging when you feel pain. When your father or mother or close friend starts to cry with you because they understand how badly you hurt, at that instant the gift of sheer encouragement binds you together.

What hurts you at this particular moment may be very small in the vast moving parade of history, but for you it needs someone who is there, someone who understands you and tries to understand how you feel. This availability for the real moment. of joy and of sorrow is the fundamental mandate of parenting and of friendship, and it turns out to be the best gift a mother or father can give their children. It means being there with love, with respect, with discipline, with tears when tears were needed and with laughter when everyone breaks out laughing.

This kind of encouragement becomes an unpayable debt— the kind every child should have the joy of owing.

C h a p t e r   1 2

Honoring Parents and Children

How does it all happen? Without our prior approval each one of us is born into the most ancient of all institutions, the family. In that relationship we grow up into our place in the world.

Our biblical faith has much to say about this ancient fellowship between children and parents. It's point of view is sometimes misunderstood, and therefore I want to explore the two key biblical texts on the subject.

Weighing Heavy
The first text is the Fifth Commandment: "Honor your father and your mother, as the LORD your God commanded you; that your days may be prolonged, and that it may go well with you,

in the land which the LORD your God gives you" (Deut 5:16). The Hebrew word for "honor" is *kabod* which means in its concrete literal sense "to weigh heavy." We are, therefore, commanded to weigh our parents heavy.

Notice that the commandment is not conditional; it is a commandment of pure grace. Through us, God intends to give "honor" to our parents. The commandment is itself good news; in fact, the word *honor* becomes the principal love word of the Law. It signals for us the grand, positive intention of God that gives meaning to the ethical imperatives of the second tablet of the Law, the ethical relationships with our neighbor.

Honored by God

The commandment, however, does not appear on an empty stage. The good news behind it is that we have ourselves been honored by God. Before he grants to us this mandate, he honors us with the first four commandments of the Torah. "I am the Lord your God who brought you out of the house of bondage." Thus the Torah begins with God's act of redemption toward his people.

The first three vertical commandments then establish a relationship between God and his people. We are set free from the need for other gods, for idols, for empty sounds. The Fourth Commandment tells us of the "cease" day in which we are to remember the God who creates (Ex 20:8-11) and who redeems (Deut 5:12-15). Since God has weighed us heavy, we now may weigh our parents heavy.

Listen to the apostle Paul as he writes to the Ephesians, commenting on this commandment: "Children, obey your parents in the Lord, for this is right. 'Honor your father and mother' (this is the first commandment with a promise), 'that it may be well with you and that you may live long on the earth.' Fathers, do not provoke your children to anger, but bring them up in the discipline and instruction of the Lord" (Eph 6:1-4).

Note that Paul adds the words "obey in the Lord" to the commandment for children, and he expands the honor mandate to include not only the honor of children toward parents but of parents toward children: "Fathers do not provoke your children . . ." Reflect for a few moments on the meaning of these two texts for our lives today.

Encouragement and Challenge

First, there is an unmistakable encouragement to each of us that is taught and implied in this commandment. We who are parents are encouraged to hear this good advice being given to our children. It has a ring of truth about it. We all also feel heartened by the word itself and especially the realization that we ourselves have been honored before we have been asked to honor others.

There is also an unmistakable challenge within the commandment. Those who are the parental recipients of honor feel the challenge that comes from the nature of the Word itself. We wonder how weighty we are. Do our children need to put their own hands on the scale to bring the weight up to a respectable level? Even though the weight is granted to us as a free gift, we still wonder about the substance of our own character. How heavy am I really?

Making Music on the Honor System

I want particularly to single out the tremendous gospel motivation that is hidden within this word *honor*. Meredith Wilson in his Broadway musical has proved to us in a whimsical way some of the possibilities of the idea of honor. *The Music Man* tells two stories side by side. First there is the story of an old-fashioned con man, "Professor" Harold Hill, who talks the people of River City into buying band uniforms and instruments for a boys' band he promises to musically train with his "think system." From this standpoint alone, the musical is wonderfully outrageous and funny. Hill has no real intention to train musicians once he has sold them the instruments and uniforms.

But there is a second, deeper story. Tommy Djilis is the bad boy in town. And Mayor Shinn who decidedly does not approve of Tommy always calls him "Ya wild kid, ya," just as some fathers always call their sons "listen." But Professor Hill calls Tommy an Assistant Band Leader; and he enlists him to help lead the boys' band. In other words, Professor Hill weighs Tommy heavier than the others in town, and in fact Tommy becomes what he is called—a leader.

Alongside Professor Hill as a central character in the musical is Winthrop, a young lad with a speech impediment He can't pronounce the letter *s*. Winthrop has a sister and mother who speak for him and are too protective, while the girl his age who cares for him has an almost impossible name for Winthrop to pronounce, Amarylis. Still Harold Hill recruits Winthrop into his band and teaches the lad to sing a song that Hill pronounces is free from the letter *s*.

Certainly, the high point of the musical is Winthrop's show-stopping song "Gary, Indiana." But the best part is that the letter *s* does appear in the song, and Winthrop sings every one of them as they come, including "Paris, France"; "Syncopation"; "Home, Sweet Home." When Winthrop was weighed heavy, if even by a "Music Man" who himself is partly a fraud, Winthrop was able to sing and talk for himself. And so we see glimpses of the profound power that is present in the word *honor*.

We have been weighed heavy by God, and that experience of grace has changed our lives permanently. By it our giftedness has been unlocked so that we too can sing every letter in the alphabet. God has used people in our lives to give to us the gift of honor just as in the Fifth commandment we are commanded to give the gift to our mothers and fathers. I believe that if the story could be told about the faith-life encounters that are present in our own separate journeys, we would hear how God has honored us so that we have become able to discover our belovedness, our gifts for ministry and our mandate for living life itself.

Hear, O Israel

Paul instructs children to obey their parents. Certainly in Paul's mind the great Hebrew word that stands behind the Greek word *obey* is the very word Moses used to call Israel to obey the Law. The word is *shema,* which literally means "to hear": "Hear, O Israel: The LORD our God is one LORD . . ." (Deut 6:4). We are to hear our parents, and this hearing (obedience) goes through a grand cycle in our lives.

The Cycle of Obedience

In the earliest years, it means submission in the most complete sense. Our very health and safety demands that very small children must totally obey and submit to the most detailed instructions of their parents. It is during the years of youth that *obey* changes its shading and meaning as a young man or woman begins moving toward independence and responsibility. There is in youth a natural and healthy straining at boundaries. The "hearing" then takes place in that more fluid setting. In adult years, the cycle may become a complete circle as aged parents find they need to obey their wiser children.

Though obedience goes through its necessary cycle of change, the mandate to honor remains. Throughout the whole journey, we are to honor, to weigh heavy, both those in the generation older and those in the generation younger.

When our three children Anne, Jon and Elizabeth were very young, I taught them to ski. In the beginning everything they knew depended on my wise and authoritative instruction. Now we have come full circle; each of them is a better skier than I and they now teach me. They watch my form and make helpful suggestions. I would be a fool not to benefit from this good and necessary change of place within the obedience cycle.

There are, however, parents who have just this problem of adult isolation and stubbornness as their sons and daughters move into adolescence. That's because they as parents are trying to relate to fourteen-year-olds as if they were seven. Living with the cycle takes skill, but the rewards are wonderful—and not only in skiing.

Honor: Our Mandate for Ministry

Let us now consider the word *honor* as our own mandate for our ministry as Christians. The commandment and Paul's commentary on it shows us that God sees each of us as members of families and not as isolated individuals. "Thy father and thy mother" are the human words not only of endearing relationship but also of historical continuity. None of us lives only to ourselves either biologically or spiritually; and this commandment points up the relational nature of our life and, therefore, of our ministry.

There is no escaping the fact that you and I are responsible for the generations on each side of our present tense. Every school and every Christian group is at that very post of responsibility as faculty and students seek to weigh heavy each student who comes into its fellowship. Each of us bears this same responsibility both toward our fathers and mothers in the faith just as we do for our fathers and mothers in physical birth. It is a rewarding responsibility but responsibility nonetheless.

Jesus Christ Weighs Us Heavy

Finally, the commandment and Paul's words show us that God

himself has intervened in our favor in the most personal of all relationships, that between children and parents. Paul uses the exciting and theologically important words *in the Lord* to stand as the larger context within which obedience is to be lived out. Our Lord has interposed his will within the family, and he has turned us loose with the grand and powerful word *honor.*

This intervention becomes the important biblical protection against child abuse or parent abuse. Because all authority between human beings is mediated in and through the intervention of the Lord Jesus Christ, no person in any family may ever argue that the authority or privacy of the family structure justifies acts which are destructive.

But here we have an even greater presence than simply mere protection: We have the presence of the Lord of honor as the positive, loving, healing, forgiving friend of our journey. We have Jesus Christ himself as the one who has done the weighing. And he has found us heavy.

Chapter 13

Weighed and Measured

There is no escape— everything and everyone is measured and evaluated. In the New Testament the Greek word for this measurement is *krino* and is translated "to judge," that is, to divide, to decide. From the moment we are born to the very end of our human journey accountability is inevitable. That's the bad news or at least it seems that way.

The good news is that there is no measuring of any life apart from the presence of the great second party, Jesus Christ. G. K. Chesterton called Jesus Christ "The Enormous Exception," the one who is our Redeemer as well as our final Judge. He is the second Adam who stands alongside each of us. The mystery of the final measuring is that Jesus Christ is both Judge and Redeemer at the same moment (Rom 8:31-39). If he were not alongside of us as our friend and advocate at the crisis of this final measurement, we would stand defeated and alone. Our wrong turns and the harm they do accumulate, and then in the measuring they lie exposed. These wrong turns are the result of our own choices, choices we made in freedom but, in the bright light of truth, we now realize were harmful.

As we reach toward Jesus Christ in faith, we also make a choice in freedom, the most significant good choice any of us ever makes. We trust in Jesus Christ who stands alongside and in our behalf and who is able to resolve the crisis caused for us by judgment—the ultimate measurement. We rightly describe that resolution by the word *salvation*. From and within the wholeness of salvation we live our life here and now as those beloved and forgiven.

Parables of Measurement

Measurement is an inevitable part of the Christian life here and now just as much as in the final sense. Jesus told many measurement parables that prove the point. He told of two houses built on two different foundations and the storms that tested them. He told about the lord of an estate who gave money to three of his workmen and then evaluated the stewardship of each employee. He told about four kinds of soil and helped us to evaluate our own life-growing patterns from the analogy of the four soils. In one way or another, every parable of Jesus may be understood as an analogy of measurement.

Five Kinds of Evaluation

Five kinds of personal evaluation are presented in the Bible, and each can play a positive role in our daily lives. Of course, testing by its very nature is unsettling, but ultimately it turns in our favor and results in our own good because of the grand purpose of the One who alone has the privilege of ultimate measurement.

First, there is the testing of my most *basic choices* about God himself and my trust or lack of trust in his faithfulness. These primary choices set the course of my life, and each one of these decisions is itself tested both by my own life experiences and by God. "For God so loved the world that he gave his only Son, that whoever believes in him should not perish but have eternal life" (Jn 3:16). This promise is a great word of hope for us, but it also sets up a profound testing of our choices.

At another level there is the evaluation of my *work*, the things that I do and make. We want to hear, as did the faithful man in Jesus' story, "Well done, good servant! Because you have been faithful in a very little, you shall have authority over ten cities" (Lk 19:17).

I am also evaluated in relation to my *gifts:* "Now concerning spiritual gifts, brethren, I do not want you to be uninformed" (1 Cor 12:1). As the result of evaluation by a fellowship of brothers and sisters who know who I am and what I do best, a certain giftedness is confirmed in my life. This evaluation may be formal or informal; in either case it has life-changing consequences.

My future *potential* is also evaluated. That takes place when those who know me encourage me to go to college or to pursue a sport because they recognize in me the possibility of success. As Paul tells Timothy, "Fulfil your ministry" (2 Tim 4:5).

Finally, as a *person in relationship* with myself and other people, I am evaluated every day in a hundred subtle and obvious ways. Barnabas "was a good man," writes Luke, "full of the Holy Spirit and of faith" (Acts 11:24).

Stress and Strain
Just knowing about these five kinds of evaluation and knowing

they are inevitable makes it easier to take S.A.T. tests, to submit to job performance evaluations, or even to face a physical examination with blood work and a stress E.K.G. In fact, the one common thread in all evaluations is that by their very nature they produce stress and make us feel uncomfortable. Jesus, knowing what he would do to solve the problem, asked Philip how their small band could be expected to feed the multitude: " 'How are we to buy bread, so that these people may eat?' This [Jesus] said to test him" (Jn 6:5-6).

T. S. Eliot's "The Love Song of J. Alfred Prufrock" is a poem in which Prufrock is tested and found wanting, most of all by himself.

There will be time . . .

. . . yet for a hundred decisions and indecisions,
And for a hundred visions and revisions. . . .
I have measured out my life with coffee spoons. . . .
So how should I presume? . . .
Then how should I begin
To spit out all the butt-ends of my days and ways?

Despite the potential for discouragement, the stress produced by the five evaluations I have described is good, provided we neither underrate nor overrate their importance. The only way to hold the right balance is to (1) learn from the evaluation, (2) do what needs to be done because of what we have learned and then (3) get on with our lives.

What do I need to learn? What do I need to do? And how do I get on with my life without becoming trapped in the process of endless testings? These are the three most important questions.

Learning from Evaluation

Learning happens when I am open to discovery. So I need to listen to the various critics of my life who in one way or another are evaluating my fundamental values, my personality, my giftedness, my potential and my work.

It is not always easy to be open because we are all so naturally self-protective. We don't want stress. Even the most apparently routine evaluation moves toward the center of my self-understanding and my self-confidence. Who am I? What am I worth? If I am sensitive—and most of us are—the answers can be frightening.

Because all human beings are so vulnerable, it is important that as evaluators of other people we become wise and skillful in giving critical feedback to others. Evaluation of a young pastor's work, of a teen-ager's musical potential, of a friend's physical appearance can either encourage or damage self-confidence. The influence that accompanies a friend's or counselor's estimate of our abilities or our character is often remarkably forceful.

I remember Mr. Dallas Birch, an older man who was a great friend to my brother and me while we were growing up. When I was in junior high, he had an unusual molding influence in my life, both spiritually as my Sunday-school teacher and in other ways too. For example, he was himself a superior card player, the best I've ever known, and he taught my brother and me how to play various games. One evening he announced that I had an outstanding ability to remember cards that had been played. His estimate greatly strengthened the quality he noticed, and I believe it is one of the reasons I still have such a good memory. Positive, creative evaluation is very influential for the development of a good self-image.

But evaluation can also pose a danger to self-confidence. As I reflect back, I think I have worried too much about my height and my weight. You see, some people during my most impressionable youthful years said I was too fat and too short, at least I thought they said so.

Responding to Evaluation

The proper response to evaluation—positive, negative or neutral—is not the fantasy strategy of isolating ourselves from the shared thoughts of other people. Instead a healthy self-balance enables us to learn, then to make moves where needed as a result of discovered insight and finally to get on with our lives. There is always something to be learned from every evaluation even if that evaluation is unfair, faulty and harmful. In the latter case, what needs learning is the unfair, incomplete and perhaps mixed-up nature of the evaluator or of the criteria used to test my life or some work I have done.

I remember when my daughter Anne, who was then a high-school senior, received her rejection notice for admission from Princeton University. She called me at work and said a little tearfully, "Well, Dad, they turned me down." I asked her how she felt about it, and she said, "Well, it hurts. But, then, I said to myself, 'Boy, they don't know what a terrific person they missed out on!' "

I was proud of Anne that afternoon because, of course, she was right. But I agreed with her most of all because to assess her potential she trusted greater foundations than an admissions committee could possibly know. Since that afternoon when the thin envelope from Princeton arrived, time has proved her right.

There are no perfect evaluators except for the Judge of all the earth, and one of the first truths that should be learned from the experiences of evaluation is just this fact.

Nevertheless, inadequate or not, the testing goes on, and with every test, there is something more to learn. Naturally, we learn the most when the weighing is fairest. Clarification and realistic encouragement toward growth results from a fair test. It is important to know if a math set I have done has ended up with the correct answer and I have used the proper method of solving the problem. Every youth leader or pastor needs feedback from parents, and not only the warm endorsement of appreciative families but also the disappointment of hurting families who feel that their son or daughter has somehow fallen through the cracks of the ministry program. In each case, however, when I am evaluated, I learn about five freedom areas of my life.

Getting On with Our Lives

The next step is to do what must be done with what I have learned. I may need the healthy experience of repentance. I may need to take corrective measures to solve a crisis that is now clear to me as a result of an evaluation. But there is the wonderfully opposite possibility too: I may have discovered I have a gift I didn't know about. Those who were watching me saw real talents and skills that I will now put to work.

One day, however, the bell rings and the exam is over at least for now. Testing cannot go on forever, and there comes a moment when each of us must know how to relax and trust ourselves to the grace of our advocate, Jesus Christ. "But by the grace of God I am what I am" (1 Cor 15:10). St. Paul who wrote these words to the Corinthians fully understood the need for the check and balance of evaluation on his life, his work and his convictions (see Galatians 1—2). Then in summing up his reflections on criticism he has been receiving, he says, "Henceforth let no man trouble me" (Gal 6:17). He realized that evaluation must not become a permanent pause in which action continually awaits one more evaluative process or study to be completed and tabulated.

I know of churches and schools and people who have choked off their ability to make worthwhile decisions because of continual studies, surveys and evaluations. They keep searching for clues they will never find because no one gets on with the job of living out the gospel as it is understood right now.

Steering a Car in Motion

Henrietta Mears's proverb is still accurate and helpful to me: "You can't steer a parked car. Let's get it moving and then we can see where to steer." There are no flawless moves; and therefore, we need the testing of our lives and our work. But for that very reason we must not rely too much on our weighing of the life and work of another person or of ourselves. After all, God can cope with our mistakes just as he copes with our successes. We want to be, in the good sense, reactive to the evidence of evaluation so that we learn from evaluation, but we must also take the risk of getting on with the work we need to do. We must be pro-active too.

We should risk the testing of our five freedoms for which we have a fivefold accountability. But we must also risk getting on with our lives and then to feel good about it because the final accountability is in the hands of the One who knows us best and stands alongside us at every moment.

Chapter 14

"I Take Hands Off"

During his freshman year at Yale University, William Borden wrote this prayer in his journal: "Lord Jesus, I take hands off, as far as my life is concerned. I put thee on the throne of my heart. Change, cleanse, use me as thou shalt choose. I take the full power of thy Holy Spirit. I thank thee."

This faith event changed William Borden's life and set in motion a shift of direction that had a profound effect on his student years at Yale and Princeton Seminary and on his brief career as a missionary to Egypt. Borden died in Cairo of cerebral meningitis at the age of twenty-five. His life was short but fully lived. His commitment to Jesus Christ and the world missionary mandate of the gospel still continues to challenge those of us who know his story.

"I Take Hands Off"

Only a narrow, fragile line divides active commitment from apathy. In both, we experience something that could be described in Borden's words: "I take hands off."

Isn't it remarkable? The same brief sentence, "I take hands off," is the key opening thought both for strong, motivated action and for the demotivation of all action. How can this be? In both instances, there is a "taking hands off" as a person realizes the limitations of human power; in both there is a disillusionment with achievement and human success; in both there is a feeling of letdown because people have fallen short of our hopes for them. But what makes the difference is what we do with these feelings of disappointment, inadequacy or fatigue.

These feelings go through my mind when I have just failed to really make a go of a project that was important to me. My own missed opportunity, the stonewalling of my coworkers, whatever the reason, I know in my heart that I am standing on an edge. Everything must pause. I have loosened my grip because there is nothing else I can do.

I have had this feeling right in the middle of committee meetings; I have had it as a parent and as a marriage partner. At some of those failure moments I was supposed to stand tall as a father/husband/son. I felt it especially at times when I was misunderstood.

I also get the feeling when I know I have "dropped the ball" as a pastor/teacher. At those key moments I am standing at a pause, at a time between the times. The important question is this: Which way do I go now?

Standing between the Times

As a young man Borden stood at such a time between the times. Borden puts it in a straightforward way in his journal entry. He knows himself well enough not to place himself or his successes or his defeats at the center of his life—"on the throne of [his] heart." This is why he took hands off.

He knew only too well the inadequacy of the people and institutions around him. Not his church, nor his school nor any set of idealistic programs or slogans could be put on the throne of his heart. He chose Jesus Christ as the living center for his life. He decided to live under Christ's will, and he claimed the assurance of the Holy Spirit.

This act in favor of life and his part in it made all the difference. It was not a decision that lessened his problems or answered all his questions. Undoubtedly he had more issues and questions and doorways to enter than before. The difference is that he was under way on a journey under grace.

Away from Pathos
Apathy has the same early building blocks and agrees with the same opening sentence of Borden's prayer. Apathy also "takes hands off," but it stops there with almost nothing more, almost nothing else. It takes hands off because it settles in with the feeling of letdown and therefore institutionalizes disappointment.

Until the soul settles down, apparently relaxing all effort at deciding, there is a ring of truth, a necessary discovery process that has been under way. But something gives out, and the soul decides to stop deciding! This is what apathy is (it is what the word means: a-pathos, "away from pathos," "away from suffering or strong experience"). Apathy takes hands off as far as everything that might happen is concerned.

The Choice for No Choice
There is a double irony in apathy as a "choice" for no choice. The first is that all human choices against strong feelings and

the involvements that go with feelings will nevertheless inevitably produce a large collection of inner feelings, some low-grade (like nonaggressive cynicism) and some very intense (like depression). We find out that we cannot escape pathos by deciding against pathos.

The second irony is that the most common reason given for apathy is fatigue. The most familiar arguments for not caring and not trying are "I'm too tired to care anymore," or "I've had it" or "I'm burned out." But the evidence is clear that apathy uses up more emotional and physical energy than either action or hope.

Now for the bad news: Apathy as a protection against further fatigue is like the reasoning in favor of smoking clove cigarettes to soothe a raw throat. The relief is totally imaginary. The basic irritation in the throat is actually becoming worse since the cloves have a side effect that blocks the pain which is the body's way of alerting us to the destruction that is under way though undetected.

A Filter for the Soul
There are no easy solutions to apathy when it happens in us, especially if we become used to the gray comfort which blurs all hard choices, hides all real suffering and all real joy from us. Like dark sunglasses, apathy is a filter for the soul. Once we get used to the grayness of noninvolvement, the one advantage of apathy—that it cuts down the glare of pain—is hard to unlearn.

Who are apathetic people? Nondeciders are sometimes disappointed idealists who once had high hopes either in themselves or in a certain cause or ideal. When the ideal appears to collapse, or even to shake a little because of stress, they withdraw and decide to refuse to decide on all really costly future issues as a protection against what they think will be progressive disappointment. But this hands-off cure for disappointment actually is the source of the worst of all forms of disappointment—the dull cumulative loss of interest in life itself.

Taking the Cure

Is there a cure and, if so, what is it? We can be thankful that because God exists there is a cure for everything including such a complicated life pattern as apathy and all of its companion nonpossibilities. It happens in stages for most people, but finally it requires us to take the dark glasses off and join the rest of the human race. It requires us to decide to decide. The cure draws us into the rich colors of human feeling and risk taking where the rewards are better than the possible dangers.

Best of all, the cure calls us to enter into fellowship with the nonapathetic Lord of life. All of this takes time, but that's one of the best parts of the cure.

May we, then, pray with William Borden: "Lord Jesus, I take hands off, as far as my life is concerned. I put thee on the throne of my heart. Change, cleanse, use me as thou shalt choose. I take the full power of thy Holy Spirit. I thank thee."

Afterword

It is not hard to be a twenty-four-hour Christian because God sleeps lightly.

If we were to live the Christian life through our own mastery of spiritual principles, we should have two equal dangers—the feeling of disappointment when we failed to achieve the principles, and the layer of deception when we felt we had succeeded.

Christian faith is not an *ideal* but a *divine reality*, to use Bonhoeffer's terms in *Life Together*. And it is the realism of Christian faith that makes it both difficult and good at the same time. We are never through growing because of the greatness of the call to walk with Jesus and obey his will for our lives. Because of that immense call we always need forgiveness and help.

But the one who calls us to follow is a friend who knows us better than we know ourselves. He is the source of our life and the companion of our journey throughout the whole twenty-four hours. Each day is another beginning. We can join in at any hour—very early or very late, at night or midday—better early than late. The most important of times is now.

Printed in the United States
1082800001B/472-492

9 781573 832229